Kultitja

Linda Wells

Kultitja
Memoir of an outback schoolteacher

Acknowledgements

Sincere thanks to the following people:

Greg Bastian, who encouraged me to write this memoir and was hugely helpful in its development, including invaluable editorial assistance.

Mac and Maralyn – generous and supportive always.

Marly, who challenges me, makes me laugh and keeps things real.

Bernadette Young, the Sweeney-Calverts of Northcote and Cherrie Eaton, who all provided me with spaces that enabled me to concentrate on my writing.

Staff and fellow students in the Swinburne postgraduate Arts/Writing program who also provided invaluable feedback.

Margaret Gee for believing in my work.

And special thanks to the kind, generous people of Mount Allan.

Not everything in this memoir is exactly as it occurred, but everything is told totally in the spirit of what happened. Some names have been changed to protect people.

Kultitja: memoir of an outback schoolteacher
ISBN 978 1 76041 125 1
Copyright © Linda Wells 2016

First published 2016 by
GINNINDERRA PRESS
PO Box 3461 Port Adelaide 5015
www.ginninderrapress.com.au

You walk out into that landscape and there's no sign of man. It's a big sky and big landscape that suits big emotions… You can find God and the spirit of the land and see yourself as a pretty insignificant dot in the universe.

Shane Howard

For Maureen and Brenda

1

I drove out of Alice Springs just after dawn, the sun a huge fiery ball on the horizon. Twenty kilometres along, I turned left and travelled, due west. My old blue Holden purred along, loving the free run. I wound down the window, turned the stereo up and sang at the top of my voice. It amazed me how quickly I could leave it all behind.

*

I'd been in Central Australia for six weeks by then, up from a brief stint living in Tasmania. That's where I'd met Yacca, a part-wild fella who lived in a hut in the forest.

'I've got some friends in Alice Springs,' he'd said to me. 'Do you want to come and meet them?'

Gypsy by nature and curious beyond cure, I had jumped at the chance.

Yacca's friends were the Buzzacotts, an Arrernte-Arabunna family who lived twenty kilometres out of town. They welcomed us and invited us to set up camp on the back of an old truck. It was immersed in stunning desert bushland. I'd never imagined the desert to be so dense and abundant. I'd never imagined living on the back of an old truck. Once there, I could imagine nothing else.

Kevin Buzzacott was a master storyteller and red-dust philosopher. Around campfires in the relative cool of each evening, Kevin rolled up smokes and entertained us with talk of the culture, of political struggles and developmental challenges. He talked rough but smart and I could have sat up listening to him all night. He was the director of Yipirinya School for Aboriginal kids in Alice Springs, passionate about the work they were doing.

'Them kids, they need an education that respects who they are. But we gotta teach 'em mainstream too. Two-way education, two ways of language, two ways of culture. The government's not gonna do it. They got their own agenda. We gotta do it ourselves.'

'Do you need any teachers? Could I work there?'

Kevin told me Yipirinya School was only employing teachers who had experience in Aboriginal education. 'If you wanna get involved, get yourself a job out bush. Find out what it's all about. Them mob out bush, poor bastards, they're cryin' out for teachers.'

In the Education Department office, they signed me up right away. They had a job for me beginning in a couple of weeks.

*

I thudded from the bitumen onto the dirt at the threshold between one world and another. 'Careful driving techniques are advised', read the road sign, too stark; too white against the desert backdrop. What on earth could they be I wondered.

Where the bitumen met the dirt, I pulled over to the side of the road and turned off the engine. I pushed open the creaking door, stepped out and strolled over to stand in the middle of the Tanami Highway. It was smooth and black the way I had come, a scar slicing through the wilderness. And corrugated dirt where I was headed, the rusted colour of the desert floor.

The morning sun cut into me, flies buzzed around my face. I stood, spellbound by the landscape. Desert plains overgrown with low, scrubby bushland. Ancient ranges rising in the distance. A lone eagle soared overhead, from deep blue to burnt orange where the sky met the sun-drenched land. It was still and silent as if everything had been that way, unmoved, for aeons. And clingingly hot, like a blanket that moved in around you and wouldn't be shaken off.

I grew to know that desert scenery the more time I spent with it. Like the back of my hand, like my own backyard. But it's not the landscape I remember most from that first day. It's how I felt. The awe and anticipation. The strangeness.

There was nothing coming for the miles I could see in either direction. I hitched up my skirt and squatted, delighting in the freedom. My piss frothed as it hit the ground and made a little pool in the soft red earth before trickling away.

Behind the wheel again, I had the new sensation of bumping over unmade road, gripping the wheel and steering it cautiously over corrugations that threatened to throw me off track. Thick clouds of red dust poured out behind. In front the road forged, still and straight, further and further in.

I pictured the photos I'd seen in the Education Department office: big glossy prints on display, of velvet brown children with endearing smiles, books held upside down on their laps. A scattering of simple dwellings, figures seated beside campfires. The desert splashed behind.

'Wow. That place looks fantastic,' I had told the superintendent who was overseeing my appointment.

'Rough conditions out there, girlie,' he growled.

I wondered, was there something about me he particularly disliked or was he this dry and gruff with everyone?

'All the better,' I replied and he shot me a look of disgust. I suppose he'd heard it all before. Young woman from the south, off for a little adventure with the natives. I found out later the average stay for a teacher in those parts was three months.

'Shorts won't be suitable. They wear skirts out there,' he continued, as if I'd already done something wrong. 'The women dress discreetly, they behave discreetly too.'

'When in Rome…' I replied and he nodded.

As his parting gift he offered, 'The head teacher is Alastair Burns. You two should get along.'

*

Tilmouth Roadhouse loomed up like some strange phenomenon from outer space, crash-landed on the hinterland between desert plain and sandy river bed. As did the manager.

'Oh, you're the new teacher for Mount Allan, are yer? Goin' out to teach them black fellas somethin'. Well, good luck, darlin'.'

'No, actually I'm going to learn things from them.'

'What? How to drink and sit around? You'll find out, love.'

'We'll see.' I shrugged and turned away.

I wandered down to the river, a short stroll from the roadhouse. Napperby Creek, the sign said. It defied any notion of creek I'd ever had. In my life until then, a creek had been a narrow ditch of gurgling brown water. This one was broad, apparently with no water and dotted with river red gum trees that seemed to grow up out of the sandy river base.

In the shade of one of those river red gums, I stretched my muscles, stiff from driving, then plonked onto the sand. It was soft and gritty and felt good to sit on and run my fingers through. The tree before me was sprawling and gnarled and hosted a variety of life; ants made tracks along the smooth bark of the trunk, Galapagos-looking beetles ran this way and that, birds tweeted from the overhead canopy and poked their little heads out from knots along the trunk.

I thought back to studies I'd done as part of my year 11 biology course, of how those river red gums supported myriads of life, each an ecosystem of its own. Of how dry sandy river beds like Napperby Creek became raging torrents after rain. Of plants and animals with their finely honed adaptations that came alive to make whoopee and scatter their seed then retreat back to moister, dark places before the world dried out again.

From my study desk in the suburban south, such places had seemed wondrous and out of reach. In my second last year of high school, I was booked onto a school bus trip to Alice Springs and Uluru. Not long before we were due to go, I cut my foot quite badly on the science room door and was walking with the aid of crutches. I was welcome to still go on the trip and for others to carry my bag and pitch my tent. But I didn't want to go to Central Australia under those conditions. I wanted to carry my own bag and pitch my own tent. The road less travelled. Off the beaten track. I guess that's the way I've always been.

On that long and corrugated road again, sometimes I saw things that turned out to be not there. Mirages. Old black men standing tall on one leg that turned into trees. Kangaroos that morphed into rocks.

I could see something up ahead. A car parked by the side of the road. Some dark figures milling around. As I got closer, it didn't change form but became more defined: a battered old twin-cab ute, parked in the dust and jacked up at one corner. Nearby, a group of people were squeezed into the shade of a couple of mulga bushes.

I slowed down to take in the scene, wondering what to do. I was tempted to stop but I was unsure of bush protocol. Was I intruding? Was I safe? Would they even understand me? Poor bastards, Kevin Buzzacott had called them.

There were men whose faces were partially hidden beneath battered Akubra hats, women sitting cross-legged in loose skirts. In the lap of one of the women a plump, brown baby slept, wrapped only in a disposable nappy. Children eyed me curiously before looking away. They must be like the kids I was going to work with, I thought: big brown eyes, long skinny limbs and sun-bleached hair that stuck out from their head in tufts.

The older of the men heaved himself up from his resting place and started to cross the road towards me. He wore shorts and a button up shirt, loose and crumpled. His face was weathered, with broad features and a soft-looking grey beard.

'Hello,' I called out, through my open window.

'Allo,' he replied and I suddenly felt much more at ease.

I paused, unsure what to say next, not wanting to seem trite or invasive.

'You right?' he asked me, now standing a metre from my window but facing up the road.

I smiled. Of course that's the thing to say. 'Yes, thank you. Are you all right?' I opened the door and stepped out.

'Yeah, we right,' he replied. He turned back to look at the others, as if making sure. Then he nodded and added, 'Where you headed?'

'Mount Allan.'

'Moundallan,' he repeated.

'Yes, Mount Allan. You know it?'

'Yeah we know Moundallan,' he replied, grinning. 'You must be new *Kultitja*.'

I looked at him, puzzled.

'*Kultitja*, you must be new *Kultitja*.'

I shook my head.

The younger man walked towards us. He was tall and wiry, dressed like an outback cowboy: trousers, a shirt and heeled boots that looked way too hot for the day. He tipped his tall black hat politely. '*Kultitja*,' he repeated, slowly and carefully. 'You coming to be *Kultitja* for Moundallan?'

The penny finally dropped. 'Oh, schoolteacher,' I blurted out.

'*Yuwayi, Kultitja.*'

We laughed, the young man and the old man and myself. The people in the shade weren't looking but some of them were smiling too.

The younger man spoke again. 'I'm Kelbin Paterson. Eberyone call me KP. This old man, he my father, Shorty Paterson. We from Moundallan community.'

We shook hands in a way that was more like a gentle holding than the pumping or squeezing I knew to be a handshake. I shook Shorty's hand too.

I told them my name and in response KP said, 'You right, you welcome.'

'Do you need any help?' I asked them.

'Nah. We're waitin' for that other mob to come back from Tilmouth Well, that roadhouse up the track. They took our tyre to fix 'im up. We got no pump. You got 'im pump?'

'No,' I replied, shaking my head.

'Well, look out,' KP replied jovially. 'You might get 'im puncha?'

KP and Shorty laughed at this, along with some of the others on the side of the road.

It took me a moment and then I laughed too. 'I have a spare tyre,' I announced and they nodded sagely.

One of the women called out something I couldn't possibly understand.

KP asked me, 'Eberything all right?'

I figured the woman had prompted his asking. He looked at my car and then back at me. I looked from KP to Shorty, to all of the other people in their party, all from one car, roughly the same size as mine except they had the tray back, and I could only guess how they might be seeing me.

'Yeah, I'm right.'

'You want compny?' KP asked in a way that seemed kind and curious.

I would have loved company. I would have loved some of those calm looking women and their skinny, life-charged children to come with me and introduce me to their country. I thought of my boot and my back seat and half the front seat full of the clothes and books and kitchenware I'd brought along to help cushion the fall into my new world. Right now they were just in the way.

'My car's full,' I told him and wondered if he'd have any idea what I might mean.

'Oh, you're right then?'

He nodded but I felt frustrated, like I wanted him to understand my predicament but I didn't know how to get him to.

I rifled through my boxes and bags and found some oranges and a bottle of water and handed them to KP. 'Here, for your wait.'

I was struck by the sincerity of his thanks.

'Dribe carepully.'

Everyone waved as I drove slowly off so as not to shower them with dust and stones. I was bursting with joy.

*

It's a different kind of highway where you can travel for hundreds of kilometres, barely passing another vehicle. Where the road is lined on either side by wilderness, in every direction, for what seems like eternity. Where broken-down cars have been abandoned in the bush, frequently turned on their heads, to rust and rot and scar the landscape during their long dissolution. Where huge eagles soar overhead and swoop down suddenly for roadkill. The Tanami Highway was like no other I had known.

Another one hundred and eighty kilometres of corrugated road, with the odd car going the other way. We waved each time; highway solidarity. Then a sign pockmarked with bullet holes: 'Mount Allan Store 60 km.' The Mount Allan road was not quite as wide as the Tanami but similar in all other respects. I bounced along this, the final stretch.

Suddenly the landscape changed: a maze of rough tracks forged into the bush, a surprising amount of litter scattered across the ground. Then round a bend, over a hill and suddenly Mount Allan. It seemed like a most unlikely place to come across a village, and I was thrilled that I finally had.

A large expanse of water to my left took me by surprise. It was a dam, glinting in the afternoon sun; a significant water feature in an otherwise arid landscape.

I turned right, away from the dam, onto a short road that appeared to house the central business district. On one side of the road were official buildings with vacant land in between. Council Office, Community Store, Yuelamu Art Centre. I read the signs out loud like I was announcing these places to an imaginary audience.

On the other side of the street, each in its own dusty yard, was a stretch of plain, brick houses. Each yard was bare red earth with the occasional straggly tree. The road ended in a cul-de-sac, where two large square vans sat perched atop metal frames, again fenced off in adjacent yards. They were just as the superintendent had described: the teachers' accommodation.

It was Sunday afternoon and the place seemed deserted; no welcoming committee nor curious onlookers that I could see. That was okay; I could ease my way in gently.

As I pulled up outside the teachers' demountables and stepped out of the car, a man suddenly appeared. 'We've been expecting you,' he told me. 'Alastair Burns,' and he offered his hand for a shake that turned out to be another of those gentle holdings that I'd experienced back on the highway.

I wasn't used to shaking hands but this way seemed preferable to the firm pump of a businessman. I figured this was the way they did it out here: the desert shake.

Alastair was a wiry, energetic man, about forty years of age. He had the air of someone on the go. He wore cotton shorts, a button-up shirt and a wry little grin that I suspected was as much a part of him as his groomed moustache. This made me feel instantly at ease. On Alastair's feet was a pair of practical leather sandals and on his head an Akubra hat, battered and well-worn to a perfect fit. His sandals and hat were of the same ilk as ones I had bought in Alice Springs for my new remote life. It seemed I was on the right track.

Alastair was married to Ada, he told me, an Aboriginal woman from a neighbouring community, two hundred kilometres to the south. They were Luritja people over there and they spoke the Luritja language, whereas the people of Mount Allan were Warlpiri and Anmatyerre and spoke one or both of those languages.

Alastair and Ada had three young daughters: Maggie, Laati and Sharon. As we spoke that first day, those girls alternately ran around playing or clung to his legs, eyeing me shyly. They were honey-coloured, lighter-skinned than the kids I'd seen on the road earlier but with the same long, thin limbs, big brown eyes and golden, sun-bleached hair. I thought that I had never seen anything so cute and I wanted to play with them.

Alastair addressed the biggest of the girls. 'Maggie, say hello to the new schoolteacher, Miss Wells.'

'I'd prefer Linda,' I told him.

Maggie growled at him in words I couldn't understand then eyed me from behind him while he explained, apparently, what she had said.

'Linda is *Kumenjayi* in these parts. There was a community member by that name. She passed away. If someone passes away, they don't use that name any more. They say *Kumenjayi* instead.'

'Allo, Miss Kumenjayi,' Maggie whispered shyly, looking at her feet.

'Hello, Maggie, pleased to meet you,' I replied.

She looked up at me and met my smile then held my outstretched hand for a gentle desert shake before looking away again.

'Good girl,' said Alastair, beaming.

Miss Kumenjayi became one of my Mount Allan names.

They showed me to the big white van on a platform, elevated off the ground. A set of tin steps led to the door, which Alastair unlocked before ceremoniously handing me the key. The front door opened into the kitchen. At the far end was a bedroom, at the near end a small bathroom and laundry. The place was minimally but adequately furnished: a brand-new inner-spring mattress, a table and chair set, a fridge and washing machine, all reasonably new and in good repair. The walls were lined with a thin wood panelling. On the kitchen wall was a large, white unit that Alastair told me was the air conditioner. I'd never lived with one of them before. The whole place seemed clean, fresh and entirely liveable.

Alastair left me to settle in. A while later, I heard him calling his daughters home to dinner. I grinned at the suburban neighbourliness of it, out here in the middle of nowhere. Their silver bullet next door looked larger and more shaded.

'It's rough conditions out there,' I said out loud, mimicking the superintendent. It seemed luxurious compared with other accommodation I'd paid for through my life – the dingy student digs in St Kilda, the dark cottage atop the Strzelecki ranges. 'Rough conditions,' I gasped as I stood in the open doorway, drinking in the vast array of stars that were appearing in the night sky. On first appearances, conditions didn't seem too rough at all.

2

Sleep came slowly that first night. It was hot, like someone had turned the heater on way back and never bothered to turn it off. I tossed and turned then remembered the air conditioner and figured out how to switch it on. I'd never used an air conditioner before. It blew cool air but rattled noisily against the wall. I couldn't sleep with that racket. I turned it off and lay sweating again. Eventually I located a towel and wet it down in the bathtub. With that draped over my body, I finally drifted off.

I woke early, surprisingly refreshed. Nothing, not even a short, overheated night's sleep could curtail my excitement. Through my window I witnessed the sun coming up, that huge dazzling ball.

The kettle, Linda Electric, amused me. Blackened billycan on crackling fire was how I imagined I would make tea in my new desert life. Instead I found aspects of middle suburbia set amongst ancient earth worship. The merger never ceased to amuse.

People started moving around, walking down the road at a short distance from my home. I peered out the window, half expecting a mob to be looking my way, waiting for me to emerge. There was that sheer blue sky, the bare red earth and the scrappy makeshift look of a village in the middle of nowhere. Of the people that were going by, on their own or in small groups, no one seemed the least bit interested in me.

Where were they going, I wondered, this early in the day. What were their names? Where did they sleep? What were they talking about? There were people on their own, people in small groups, those ragamuffin-looking children. I was bursting with curiosity and dying to get out amongst my new community. At the same time, I felt shy and alien.

Alastair appeared at the bottom of my steps. I heard him calling out to me long before he arrived.

'Morning, Miss Kumenjayi… Time for school.'

He appeared as he had the evening before, buoyant and energetic, in cotton shorts and shirt, with his Akubra hat sat snugly upon his head. I wondered if he wore it to bed.

I was wearing a free-flowing skirt that sat just above the knee, a plain T-shirt and my own pre-loved Akubra. 'When in Rome,' I said to myself, and thought of my prickly old superintendent.

I hoisted myself up into the front cabin of the Toyota four-wheel drive, feeling like a truckie chick. It was the Pulardi Outstation vehicle, provided by the Education Department, which I would be in charge of from now on.

'You be right with this?' Alastair asked.

All that size and grunt and nothing like I had driven before. 'You bet,' I replied without hesitation.

Alastair cruised slowly down the main drag. The first building to our right was the art centre.

'What's the name of the centre?' I asked.

'Oh, Yuelamu. That's the official Aboriginal name for Mount Allan.'

'So is that what we should call it?'

Alastair shrugged. 'It depends who you're talking to.'

The tin shed next to that was the Mount Allan store.

'It's a typical bush store,' Alastair told me, shaking his head. 'They're all the same. Rubbish food, too expensive. It's one of the problems out here. Stock up when you go to town and you can get your box of perishables flown in once a week. You know about that, don't you?'

I told him I did. As an incentive for teachers to work out bush, the Education Department covered the freight costs for a weekly supply of fresh food to be flown out from town.

Some people sat outside the store.

Alastair waved to them out his open window. 'Morning, Mick,' he called to a solid-looking young man.

Mick maintained a poker face but gave a generous wave in return.

'Morning, Jilpi,' Alastair then called to an older, wizened man who was seated on a patch of grass beside a much younger woman.

The old man gave a small wave and a nod.

'That's old Jack with one of his wives,' Alastair told me.

'Jack. But what did you call him?' I asked. 'Jil...?'

'Oh, Jilpi.' He smiled. 'That means old man.'

'Old man? Do you call him that to his face?'

Alastair grinned and nodded. 'In the traditional way, old people are respected. He's proud to be a Jilpi.'

'Did you say she was *one* of his wives?' I asked, craning my neck to look back at the pretty woman seated beside old Jack. 'How many does he have?'

'Three,' Alastair replied. 'Most of them only have one these days but Jack's following the old way. He's got an old wife his age, a middle-aged one and then that young one.'

'Do they have kids?' I asked.

'Oh yes, a few kids with each of them. Some of his kids are grown-up. And he's got some young ones that come to school.'

'Wow,' was all I could manage in response.

Alastair pointed out a rundown house, opposite the store. 'The grand old homestead,' he announced.

In my romanticised view of outback Australia, homesteads were solid and gracious establishments at the end of long tree-lined avenues. This one didn't look like an old homestead to me, just a flimsy, dilapidated shack. What was a homestead doing out here anyway, in the middle of an Aboriginal settlement?

'Mount Allan was a cattle station first,' Alastair explained. 'It was set up by Whitefellas, D.D. Smith's family. The local people are running it these days.'

'Who lives in the homestead now?'

'Oh, old D.D. comes and goes. They've kept him on as an adviser. The people here like him. Sometimes he loans them money and when people go to town he lets them stay on his back lawn.'

'Do you like him?' I asked, feeling cynical about a cowboy loan shark who put people up on his back lawn and thought he was doing them a favour.

'It's not up to me,' Alastair shrugged.

We continued down the dusty street, past a couple more houses on the homestead side and vacant land on the other. At the end of the vacant land was a plain, square, brick building.

'Operation central,' Alastair said with his wry grin. 'With Janice at the helm – she who must be obeyed. Janice makes the rules and the rest of us follow along as best we can. Go and introduce yourself to her later on. She'll be pleased to meet you and she'll tell you all about it, everything you need to know. One of her many roles is to sort the mail, so we have to try and stay on her good side.'

At the end of the road, he turned right to go over the hill and onto the other side.

'We are now leaving the Whitefella side,' Alastair explained in mock tour guide voice. 'Most of the *yapa* live over here.'

'*Yapa?*' I asked.

'That's the local name people use to refer to themselves. *Yapa* means Aboriginal. And they call us *kardiya*.'

'*Yapa* and *kardiya*,' I repeated carefully and he confirmed that I'd got it right.

Alastair drove slowly along the main dirt thoroughfare that was dotted with several houses. He then turned a corner onto a similar dirt road that took us to the school. Off that were many smaller tracks that led to more homes and camps where people were stirring. Wire fencing separated one yard from the next.

Accommodation seemed to range from piles of stuff on the ground which turned out to be people and their belongings, to car bodies, caravans, horse floats, shelters constructed of corrugated iron and then solid houses of brick and concrete. Some residences looked like the town dump, swathed in the refuse of daily living. Others, with their neatly raked red earth, painted garden rocks and pretty flower beds were sure candidates for tidy towns awards.

Rubbish was strewn across the ground, through some people's yards then down the tracks and roads and out into the bush. I'd seen quite a bit of rubbish along the highway too: disposable nappies, food and drink packaging, plastic bags. I hadn't expected to see so much rubbish. Weren't these people the true environmentalists, living in harmony with the natural environment? Why did they have so much rubbish on their land?

I took in as much as I could through the car window, wanting to see it all but not wanting to gawk and intrude. I was fascinated by these desert people and how they went about their business, with the council office full of imposed rules and regulations on one side and the ancient laws and ways of the desert on the other.

Right on the far edge of the community, we pulled up at the school gate, held shut with an ocky strap.

'The seat of knowledge,' Alastair announced.

Two huge demountable vans, about twice as big as the ones we lived in, were set parallel to one another in the middle of yard. There was a smaller van too, alongside one fence. That turned out to be the ablutions block. The yard was mostly desert floor with a couple of tall sprawling cedar trees that provided generous amounts of shade and scattered their little berries everywhere. There were many saplings too which Alastair told me he and my predecessor along with the kids had planted a while back. Near one of the demountables was a flagpole surrounded by a small, struggling vegetable garden. Outside the ablutions block was a washing line, bent out of shape that obviously doubled as monkey bars. A low wire fence formed a boundary between the schoolyard and community life. To me, it all seemed appropriately improvised and transitory.

Alastair picked up a couple of pieces of rubbish that had landed in the school grounds. Otherwise the yard was neat and clean, except for the cedar berries.

'We try to keep the grounds clean,' Alastair told me. 'Mount Allan school isn't a rubbish place.'

Here was the opening I needed. 'How come there's so much rubbish in the community?' I asked.

Alastair smiled knowingly. 'It's not what you'd expect, is it?'

I shook my head.

'Traditionally, they didn't have rubbish,' he continued. The closest thing to rubbish was animal bones that they threw away after a feed. They reused everything and anything they did throw away went back into the land. That's just the way it was. Now there's all this Whitefella rubbish but the people out here still treat it in the way they used to treat rubbish.'

'But it doesn't just break down any more?' I sort of asked, confused.

Alastair shrugged. 'I know that,' he replied, grinning. 'You know that. The trick is to convince everyone else. There's a lot out here that's not how you think it should be. They're not the perfect environmentalists that people on the eastern seaboard like to think they are. The noble savages. It's more complicated than that. Anyway, wait till you go to some of other communities around here,' he continued. 'Mount Allan's much better off than they are.'

I listened and took it all in, feeling like a naïve southerner with so much to learn.

'We mostly just use this demountable,' Alastair explained as we climbed a set of stairs and he unlocked the door at the top.

The tin door slammed open with a gust of wind.

It was a classroom all right, but continuing in the general theme of just for now and if we must. There was a big round mat where the kids could all sit, then desks and chairs arranged in rows, facing the blackboard. Along the top of the blackboard board ran an old-fashioned alphabet frieze full of objects that would have ranged from rare to unheard of in these parts: R for rose, V for vase, X for xylophone and Z for zebra.

At the far end of that frieze, I was amazed to see the British item herself, Queen Elizabeth II, framed and mounted on the wall behind the teacher's desk. It was shocking, like seeing someone naked. Beyond that, up the far end, was a staffroom kind of section: a fridge, an electric kettle and a photocopier. A lot of objects had handmade one-word labels stuck to them: refrigerator, photocopier, door, window, desk.

Stuck up on the surfaces surrounding the blackboard was a word bank. It contained single words printed on strips of paper and arranged in alphabetical sections. Brother. Camp. Cousin. Dam. Dog. Father.

Mother. People. Sister. Town. Yesterday. They seemed like the words that would feature in the children's lives, perhaps the words they would use to write stories. Other walls featured student art works, mostly faded and curling at the edges.

Alastair watched me as I stood at the door taking in my new workplace. 'It's a bit rough,' he said, concerned and hopeful, waiting for my response.

'I love it,' I finally answered and he breathed a sigh of relief.

My eyes fell on the primary school cursive printed neatly across the long blackboard:

> Today is Friday, 3rd November 1989.
> Next week our new teacher will come.
> Her name is Miss Wells.
> We will get happy to see her.

'Get happy?' I asked.

'It's how they talk,' Alastair explained. 'They told me what they wanted to write. I wrote it up for them, then they copied it down. We call it negotiated text. It's one of the ways these kids learn to write. They come from an oral culture. They don't see much reading and writing at home. We have to teach them the concepts of literacy as well as how to read and write. And all of that in a foreign language.'

Alastair busied himself in the room while I contemplated the enormity of the task.

Here I was, a secondary-trained teacher from the eastern seaboard. I had worked for one year at a high school in Geelong with teenagers, largely disaffected by a way of schooling that bore little relation to their lives. From there I had gone to rural Tasmania, to a school comprised of the children of loggers and greenies. Subjects I had taught to those white Australian teenagers included science, maths and geography. How much could that count towards what I had now been employed to do? Suddenly I felt nervous and inadequate

'It's all new to me,' I announced as if confessing.

Alastair laughed. 'It's new to most Australians,' he replied. 'At least you've made it out here. Don't worry. You'll be fine.'

I felt like he'd summed me up and decided I would be fine. I trusted his judgement and relaxed.

Alastair turned on two air conditioners that vibrated nosily against the wood panelled walls.

He boiled the kettle and made us some tea. 'It's bore water,' he told me, 'full of minerals. High calcium content.'

That explained the specks of white floating on my black tea. It tasted okay, perhaps a touch salty. Alastair did most of the talking and I soaked it all up. It was like a crash course in remote Indigenous education, a personalised in-service.

'They have chronic hearing problems,' he told me. 'They get infections in the tubes that connect the ears, eyes and nose. They've got this constant green snot and their ears block up. We have to get them to blow their noses a lot. That helps to clear it out. My girls are the same. They don't all live with their parents,' he went on. 'Some are cared for by aunties and uncles or their old grandparents who struggle to look after them.'

'Where are their parents?' I asked.

He shrugged. 'In town drinking. Chasing new love affairs. Some of them are dead.'

'What from?' I asked, astounded. He was blowing my romantic notions sky high, of peaceful Aboriginal people living in harmony with nature and each other, against all the odds of invasion. And he was doing it in this casual way, shattering my illusions with a wave of his hand.

He shrugged. 'Drinking. Car accidents. Disease. Too many people die young out here.' He paused then continued. 'They don't come to school all the time and when they do this is what we have to work with,' indicating the makeshift educational facility around us. 'We do our best. We get some support from the Education Department. Forms to be filled out in triplicate. Staffing formulas that make it difficult to address the real needs of these kids. Yes sir, no sir, and you do the paperwork to keep them happy. It's up to us really. You just forget about that mob in town most of the time and as long as you don't make trouble, they tend to leave you alone. We're answerable to this community, that's the way I see it.'

'Does the community get involved in the school?'

Alastair smiled warmly. 'We've got Maureen. She's the assistant teacher. She's an asset. I think she's gone to town but she'll be back. Her sister Jean is the cleaner. And there's a school council that will come to meetings any time we ask.'

I asked about the curriculum, which I knew as the official guiding document of any teaching practice. I imagined I'd be studying that as my first duty.

Alastair waved his hand towards one end of the room. 'There's a copy out the back somewhere: English, maths, science, health. Like I said, you figure out what these kids need to learn. There are some other documents you might find more useful, about how to teach Indigenous kids.'

This practical, no-nonsense approach was right up my alley. 'This seems to be my kind of school,' I replied, grinning.

Alastair directed me to a partitioned-off section at one end of the room. It was a shelved storage area with art supplies, videos, sports equipment and class sets of books. There was a small selection of teaching documents too, including theory and practical ideas for remote Indigenous education as well as the official NT curriculum document, looking new and barely opened.

I rifled through the documents, hungry for what they might contain and put a few aside that held particular appeal. Generally the ones that seemed the most relevant were the local, handmade publications with titles such as *Mathematics in Aboriginal Schools* and *Wangkami, A handbook for Aboriginal Teachers*. They were guides to remote Indigenous education, locally written, for a local audience. They had a small amount of theory and lots of practical suggestions and lesson plans. The diagrams were hand-drawn and the books were bound in ways that limited their lifespan.

I came across one report. It looked homemade, with a bright yellow, cardboard cover and a simple title in black font that resembled handwriting: *The social process of Aboriginal Education in the Northern Territory*, Mitsuro Shimpo PhD. It was fabric-bound with black trim. I skimmed through and read,

> Aborigines used to live in a harsh environment as hunters and gatherers. They developed the culture and social organisation in which they were born and died. They maintained a state of equilibrium and jointly survived.
>
> After contact with non-Aborigines, Aboriginal life began to change dramatically. These nomadic people began to settle in certain places which were not necessarily their country. They were exposed to modern facilities, and their culture and social organisation began to change. Some aspects of their life were seriously affected while other aspects strongly persisted.
>
> Under these circumstances, there are indications for further social and cultural changes, which may affect the most stable aspects of their life. Aboriginal people are presently passing through a traumatic process of change…

That's what was going on here, I realised. These were people whose cast-offs had been kangaroo bones that they tossed on a macrobiotic heap only a very short time ago. Now their cast-offs were, at least to some degree, alien toxic matter. What to do with that, how to make sense? People were figuring out how to incorporate the new into a way of living that had formerly known no such thing and therefore had no social mechanism for dealing with it.

I read on.

> The school gives a sense of insecurity to Aborigines for it is a fairly active agent of non-Aboriginal authority in the Aboriginal community…

Shimpo's writing spoke to me and perhaps it could offer some of the guidance and support I needed. I put aside my new-found treasures. I'd take them away for homework.

*

Kids slowly started to arrive, peeking their cute little faces around the door frame and eyeing me shyly.

'Come in, come in,' Alastair called to them from behind his desk. 'Come in, Loretta. Come in, Blackie. Good morning, Robert. Hello, Marshall, are you coming to school today?' He spoke in an encouraging, slightly teasing kind of voice, amusing himself as he went. 'Say hello to Miss Kumenjayi.'

''Allo, Miss Kumenjayi,' each child said shyly.

'Hello,' I replied, smiling and reciprocating the shyness.

The kids milled around the room, inspecting the artwork on the walls, having a go at reading the words on display and surreptitiously checking me out.

Loretta and Blackie were freshly washed with clean clothes and hair that was wet and slicked down straight. Robert was a bit scruffier, a tall, thin boy who seemed to be the oldest of this group. Marshall was small and unkempt with short messy hair and no shoes.

'We wanna play Lego,' one of them said to Alastair.

'Good idea. You can get the Lego out,' Alastair replied, 'so Miss Kumenjayi can get to know you.'

Two of the kids ran to shelving near the mat and dragged out two big plastic containers. Amidst clatter and blocks flying everywhere they tipped the Lego contents onto the mat and sat down cross-legged to busy themselves with construction.

As more kids arrived, they stood at the doorway to sum up the scene then sat down and joined in with the activity on the mat. Their bodies seemed lithe and nimble and they sat cross-legged in a smooth, quick motion, some of them like they were double-jointed.

I stood with Alastair as he told me about the pupils.

'That's Samuel. He and Michael are brothers. Michael's like one of those all-round good students, he's good at his schoolwork, good at sport, he's got lovely manners. Poor old Samuel's got hearing problems and he misses out on a lot. Rosie there, she lives with her grandma. Her parents have gone missing. She's a sweet little thing. Oh, that's Francis coming in now. Good morning, Francis.'

Francis looked down and muttered to his feet before taking refuge with the others on the mat.

'Francis is painfully shy. He doesn't come to school much. He's one of the Taylors. They travel around a lot, from one place to the next. I think he probably goes to school on some of the other communities too, Napperby and Ti-Tree, but I'm not sure. He doesn't seem like he's had much schooling.'

After a while I joined the kids on the mat. Alastair was offering insights. At the same time, I couldn't take it all in and remember everything he was saying and I felt like the kids knew we were talking about them and might feel uncomfortable about that. I wanted to spend some time getting to know the kids and letting them get to know me.

First I sat down close to the kids and watched them. Marshall was reaching for a block that was close to me and just out of his reach. I handed it to him and we exchanged a smile. Robert was building a tower that was so tall it was starting to sway. The other kids stopped what they were doing to watch him gradually add another piece and another piece. Marshall added sound effects as the tower rocked unsteadily and eventually came crashing down. We all laughed with Marshall's final blast of noise.

One girl came over and sat herself beside me, close enough to be touching. She was thin and wore a short flared skirt and a singlet top that hung loosely from her agile shoulders. Her hair was long and messy, turning to dreadlocks in some parts and she wore no shoes. She looked up at me with big brown eyes and a shy, beautiful smile. Her cheeks were criss-crossed with lines made, I presumed, by dry scale that stood out against the brownness of her skin. I wanted to rub moisturiser into them.

'Miss Kumenjayi, we wanna play dolls,' she said softly.

'What's your name?'

'Rosina,' she whispered.

'I don't know. Ask Alastair.'

'No, you gotta call him Kumenjayi,' she said, suddenly scowling.

'Oh, is he Kumenjayi too?'

'Yeah. He's Kumenjayi and you're Kumenjayi. You gotta call him Jakamarra.'

'Jakamarra,' I repeated.

'Yeah, Jakamarra.' She pointed to me and said, 'Miss Kumenjayi,' then pointed towards him and said, 'Jakamarra.'

Jakamarra heard his name. 'Yes, Rosina,' he said.

'Nah, we wanna play dolls.'

'What do you think, Miss Kumenjayi? Will we let them have free activities until recess?'

'Yeah, yeah,' piped up some of the others, looking at me expectantly.

'Sounds good,' I replied, with no real idea.

Some of them scrambled for puzzles, some to the home corner, some to a magnetic letters board. Others stayed with the Lego, pleased because there was all the more for them now. I went from one group to the next, helping them out, asking questions and observing how things went.

A few kids were in the home corner, wrapping dolls in blankets and arranging kitchen items into shelves. Equipment included dolls that seemed to have undergone various amputations, billycans, tin cups, plastic bottles, plastic bags, sticks and rocks.

'What's this stick for?' I asked.

'For stirring, Miss Kumenjayi.' Matter-of-factly.

'What about the rock?'

'For cheeky husbands.' They all giggled then and eyed me, curious for my reaction.

I laughed along with them.

'It's good to give them free time,' Alastair told me. 'They don't have many toys at home. This free play forms the basis of children's learning in our society. Social skills. Self-directed learning. Language development. Mathematical concepts. You can't overestimate the value of these activities.'

I wasn't trained in early childhood development but as I watched those kids going about their play I could see the merit in what Alastair said. I could see that giving the pupils time for free activities wasn't necessarily just a slack option that encroached on time for real learning. It was a legitimate part of the program through which learning took place, especially if the teachers mingled with the students and enhanced the learning opportunities.

I'd seen a book in the resource collection called *Play Based Learning*. I grabbed that and added it to my pile. I had so much to learn.

*

Later that day, I was sitting in the outdoor living space in the corner of my yard. It was an area bordered on three sides by car bonnets, joined together to form a stable windbreak. While the rest of my yard was an expanse of red earth infused with prickles, the ground in this area was a thick layer of sand that must have been brought in from a nearby river bed. In the middle was a fireplace, defined by a circle of evenly sized rocks.

The sun was big and sinking low. The extreme heat of the day had subsided and a few people were moving around at a distance. I was reading the Shimpo report, cross-legged on a blanket, in my skirt of ample flair, when a woman appeared at my gate.

'Allo,' she called out to me.

I looked over to where she was standing, a tall strong figure with a shock of thick dark hair.

'I can come in?' she asked.

'Yes, come in.'

I stood and watched as my first visitor approached. I'd seen a few women since I'd been out there; the women sitting in the shade on the side of the road yesterday, a few women around the community. Mostly they glanced at me then put their heads down. They seemed sweet and shy. This woman appeared a bit different. She was dressed more smartly, in a skirt and button-up summer top that were clean and new. Her hair was well cared for and framed her dark, intelligent face. She carried an air of quiet confidence.

The woman reached out to shake my hand. 'Allo, I'm Maureen.'

'Oh, Maureen, from the school?'

'*Yuwayi*,' and she grinned. 'That means yes.'

I grinned back. 'I know that one. That's about the only word I've learnt so far.'

'Plenty time,' she replied matter-of-factly. 'We can teach you.'

We sat down on the blanket together.

'You Kumenjayi,' she said to me after a moment then wrote my name in the sand to the side of the blanket. L i n d a.

I nodded and she wiped that name away.

'We can't say that name, someone died. Not that name.' Then she wrote another name in the clean slate she had made. G l e n d a.

'Oh, someone died called that name,' I pointed to the new name she had written, 'So you can't say my name?'

'*Yuwayi*,' pleased that I had understood. 'Too many Kumenjayi around here so we call you Miss Kumenjayi.'

'And you can write Kumenjayi words but you can't say them?' I asked.

'*Yuwayi*,' she whispered, sort of sucking the word into her mouth rather than pushing it out.

I nodded and there was a pause before we spoke again. There were lots of little pauses in our conversation. They were calm and comfortable. It felt like that's how life was out here: well-paced with lots of time to reflect or just be in the moment.

'Do you have any kids?' I asked Maureen.

'*Yuwayi*, I got four kids.' She drew four lines in the sand with her finger and pointed to them as she told me about her family. 'First I got Michael. He live with family at Willowra. Then there's Jillian. She's at Yirara. You know Yirara?'

I didn't know Yirara. Maureen explained it was a secondary school in Alice Springs for kids from the bush. 'They don't do high school out here,' she told me. 'They gotta go away.'

'Is that okay?' I asked.

'*Yuwayi*. It's okay. They gotta get an education. An' I got Gwenda. She goes to school here. And Anderson.'

'What about their father?'

'No,' she replied abruptly with a quick shake of her head. Then she looked down and whispered, 'Passed away.'

I let that sink in. 'I'm sorry,' I said.

'*Yuwayi*,' she said softly. 'Last year. He come from Willowra.'

'Where's Willowra?' I asked.

'Oh, that way,' she told me, pursing her lips and nodding to the north-west.

'Is it like Mount Allan?'

'*Yuwayi*. It's a community. Warlpiri they speak there. We speak two way here, Warlpiri and Anmatyerre. You got husband?' Maureen asked me.

'No, I left my boyfriend behind. I'm single.'

Maureen nodded and looked thoughtful. 'Single's good,' she replied quietly.

The sun was setting now, gently bowing out for the day with a splash of pretty watercolours cast outward from its core.

'You got any tea?' Maureen asked.

'You mean cup of tea? Yes. Would you like a cup of tea?'

'*Yuwayi*,' Maureen replied. 'Nice, peaceful here.'

I made tea inside with Maureen keeping me company and checking out my things. I showed her some photos of where I had been living in Tasmania.

She laughed at a photo of my old blue Holden covered in snow. 'No snow around here,' she laughed. 'Just red dust.' She asked to see photos of my family and studied them intently, asking questions about my parents and siblings.

Back outside, as the sky grew dark and strewn with stars, we drank tea and grazed on a plate of snacks I'd put together. I liked this woman with her thoughtful, easy-going manner and quiet confidence. It felt like the simple words she spoke were packed with meaning. It also seemed that although we came from vastly different places and cultures there was something that ran deeper, a common humanity and womanhood that we recognised in each other.

3

Cars roamed slowly up and down the main drag. They were mostly old Holdens and Fords in various stages of disrepair: cars with no windscreens, cars without bonnets, cars that seemed to be running on only a couple of pistons or a couple of inflated tyres or held together with wire. Most cars had more people in them than I'd ever imagined fitting into one car. I thought of that dumb joke about how can you fit one hundred people into a Mini-Minor: Maxwell Smart and 99. Some of these cars looked like they really contained a hundred people. Skinny, agile kids climbed in and out the windows, brown limbs everywhere.

My old blue Holden, which had never quite fitted into Melbourne amongst the zippy, freeway cars, was a masterpiece at Mount Allan.

The first time I met Sandy Allan he asked me, 'How much your car?'

'It's not for sale,' I told him.

'No. How much your car?'

'It's not for sale.'

'No, how much your car?' he insisted.

'A million dollars,' I told him.

We laughed together then. It became a running joke.

That, outside the store, was the first thing Sandy ever said to me. He was a jolly-looking man with a kind face. He was wearing a stained white polo shirt that fell short of covering his big round belly, then trousers that sat beneath the belly. He was accompanied by a woman who was as petite as he was hefty. She had short, cropped hair that looked like she might have hacked into it herself and a lazy eye that was half closed and didn't seem to look at you properly.

Maisy was also wearing a grubby white T-shirt with 'I love London' written on it. It was of the souvenir type with a red love heart in replace of the word love. That T-shirt amused me. We were so incredibly far away from London and I wondered what she knew about that city and if she even knew what her T-shirt said.

After we laughed, Sandy introduced himself. 'I'm Sandy. This my wife Maisy.'

I did a gentle handholding with each of them and Maisy beamed at me. 'Miss Kumenjayi,' she murmured affectionately and I beamed back.

'You right here?' Sandy asked.

'Yeah, I'm good.'

At that they both nodded sagely.

'We parents for Annette,' Sandy continued.

Annette was a quiet, helpful girl who came to school regularly. As if on cue, she appeared from the store and came to stand beside her parents. 'Miss Kumenjayi,' she murmured, as her mother had done.

'Annette,' I replied. '*Ngurrdju mayi*? Are you well?'

Annette nodded and told me, '*Yuwayi*, yes,' then we all had another good laugh.

'Well, we councillors,' Sandy told me. 'You got any trouble, you come to us.'

'*Yuwayi*,' Maisy confirmed earnestly, then the three of them walked away.

*

Groups of people were gathered outside the shop, standing around or sitting cross-legged on the dirt or patches of green grass. Mostly the males of all ages sat together. Some of them wore cowboy clothes: jeans or moleskin trousers, fancy shirts, heeled boots and tall Akubras. The people of Mount Allan had a history of station work and the men wore the gear proudly.

Women sat together in a different place. Mostly they looked soft and crumpled with messy hair and clothes that were functional rather than fashionable. Some of the younger girls wore shorts or trousers but once they reached a certain age those were replaced with the more discreet dress of women. Many women wore no shoes and the soles of their feet were as tough as leather.

Babies were passed around liberally. They were brown, adorable things, plump and content with all the attention they received. Nursing mothers popped their ample breasts out for babies to suckle on at will. They often then left their breasts hanging, either in case the babe came back for more or because they forgot to put them away. The modesty women had for their bodies seemed only to apply from the waist down.

There were other, smaller clusters of people too: couples or groups sitting separately. Children ran between the various clutches, eating, drinking and collecting more money. There was chatter, calling out and laughter: Mount Allan's market scene. People eyed me shyly at first and I eyed them shyly back.

The store was housed in a big corrugated iron shed. Two bowsers stood out the front, one for petrol and one for diesel. The dirt around the bowsers was stained with splashes of petrol.

Inside, large industrial-strength fans kept the air moving and offered some semblance of temperature control. The shop was furnished with dusty tin shelves containing dusty stock: tinned, dried, salted or pickled. One section was dedicated entirely to flour – plain or self-raising, white or white, all perfectly refined into twenty-kilogram drums, ten-kilogram sacks or smaller packets for leaner times.

Freezers contained bread and meat and two kinds of kangaroo. You could choose between real-life frozen kangaroo tails or plastic replicas of kangaroo, filled with sweet red ice. There was a range of other ice confectionery as well. There was an auto section and a clothes section with limited supplies of basics at inflated desert prices.

I walked around, fascinated by this outback store. It was rough and limited but in another way it seemed miraculous that it existed here at all.

I realised a woman was watching me from behind the counter. She was short and squat with a big bust and an air of get on with it, no nonsense.

'Love your store,' I told her and I don't think she knew how to take that. I don't think I quite knew what I meant.

'Oh, you're the new schoolteacher,' she said, as though my reputation preceded me. 'My husband and I run the store. He's done a run into town today so I'm out here by myself.'

'All the way to town and back in one day?'

'Yeah.' She shrugged like that was no big deal. 'He got going early this morning. He does it most weeks.'

I nodded and imagined the strain of that long drive, in and out, on a weekly basis.

'Do any of the local people work in here?' I asked.

'Oh, we try. They're not all that reliable.'

Comments like that irked me. 'They,' like the Aboriginal people, were all the same; a conglomerate mass of blacks. When people spoke like that I would think to myself, maybe you're not trying hard enough, or maybe people don't like your attitudes or maybe you don't have systems in place that accommodate their needs. I was judgemental of the white people who lived out bush and placed them firmly into one of two camps I had established in my mind: those who were sympathetic to the Aboriginal people and therefore useful and those who weren't.

She seemed to be sizing me up too, like maybe she had similar camps in her mind, into one of which she was slotting me. 'I suppose you'll get your supplies from town,' she said, 'and have your perishables flown in. It's the best idea. Cheaper for you and you get more choice that way. They don't eat very well out here.' And then, perhaps in response to the look on my face she added, 'But you're welcome to get anything you need in here.' She continued then, not apparently speaking to anyone in particular. 'We do our best. We have limited fridge and freezer space and it costs a lot to get the supplies out here. But people seem happy with what we're doing.'

'Thanks, Marion. I'm sure I'll be seeing you round.'

'That's how it is out here,' she laughed. 'There's not many of us.'

Thank goodness for that, I thought to myself as I made my leave. 'See you,' and I gave a friendly little wave on my way out the door.

*

Down the road was the office, clean and ordered in contrast to just about everything else.

'Maryanne, tell your grandmother to come and see me about her entitlements.'

Maryanne was skinny and brown with a shock of blonde hair sticking up all over the place. 'Grandma's sick,' she stammered.

'Well, if she doesn't come and see me, her pension will be cut off.'

Maryanne backed slowly away for several steps then turned and ran.

That was Janice, as Alastair had described. She was trim, neat and pale and appeared in stark contrast to the crumpled brown desert folk I had seen.

She had short, curly hair that looked like it was permed. I wondered if she permed it herself in her little abode or had it done during trips away. Janice's brick veneer home was on one corner and the council office on the other. In her life at Mount Allan, she trod a path between the two.

She kept the office going, she told me, and looked after the money and business in general. The mail plane came each Thursday and the community mail all came in one bag. Janice sorted the mail, ready for pick up by the various organisations. We were to give her a few hours after the plane had been then pick up our mail from the office. Janice also received the money and sorted out the individual payments for community members. She and her husband Steve were employed as the CDEP coordinators.

'What is CDEP?' I asked.

'It stands for Community Development Employment Program. The funding comes from the Commonwealth. The Aborigines must work for fifteen hours a week in order to receive their dole payment. If they want to do more work, they can get top up money. They don't like to work,' she went on. 'It's not their natural way. But these days they have to. It's good for them. Oh, some of them don't do it and then it's no work, no money.' She sort of sang 'no work, no money' like a mantra she repeated often. I wanted to dislike Janice and her federally funded program. I'd placed her firmly in the other camp.

'It sounds like they're working for the dole,' I replied.

'Well, what's wrong with that?' she snapped. 'If people want to eat, they have to work.'

'People used to eat and they didn't have to work,' I said, to be irritating and controversial.

'Yes well, those days are over. If they want what the white man has to offer, they have to come some way to playing by his rules. And before you go off thinking that the people are hard done by, this community chose to have CDEP. There's money for infrastructure and there are some worthwhile projects going on here. Those big tractors, the pipelines, construction you see around the place, it's all CDEP-driven. Steve coordinates all that. They wouldn't have all that if they just got the dole. Money for nothing helps no one.'

I needed time to think about that. Nothing was as it seemed. And if the community had chosen it, then maybe it was all right.

I saw Steve driving around later, in a work ute. He had a local man in the cabin with him and they were chatting and laughing. He waved at me from a distance and later in the day when he was on his own he pulled up and leaned out the window for a chat.

'Gudday. You must be the new school teacher.' He had a strong, pleasant face, a twinkle in his eye and the general air of one of those Aussie blokes who cruised through life, generally getting what he wanted.

'That's me. How could you tell?' I replied.

'You stick out like dog's balls,' he told me and we laughed. 'I'm Steve, I coordinate the CDEP program.'

'I'm Linda. Yeah, Janice told me.'

'Oh, you've met Janice?' and he nodded as if he was having a private thought that he then moved on from. 'What do you think of the place so far?' he asked.

'It's good,' I replied, looking across to the dam, the way we were facing. 'I loved the drive out yesterday. It's beautiful country. I think I'm gonna like it here.'

'Yeah, it's not a bad place. Take people as you find them. They're not a bad bunch.'

I nodded and smiled, wondering what he really meant.

'Well, good luck,' he added. 'We're here if you need anything.'

'Thanks, Steve. See you around.'

'Sure will.' With that he gave a little wave, banged the outside of the car door and drove off, leaving me contemplate how different Steve seemed from his wife.

'She's like a big fish in a little pond,' Alastair told me when I questioned him about her later. 'In the big world, they're nothing. Little fish. They come out here and they can throw their weight around. It makes them feel big and important.'

'But why do the people out here put up with her? Why don't they kick her out and get someone more suitable?'

'Because the next person they get might be just as bad. It's a bit of a case of the devil you know being better than the one you don't. Also the people out here are patient. They watch and wait. They know she'll go eventually. And they probably like Steve. He's okay.'

'Well, why does he stay with her?'

'Who knows?' Alastair shrugged, grinning. 'The mysteries of the human relationship. Maybe she keeps him in line. Some blokes like that.' Seeing my look of frustration, he added, 'You just have to sit back and wait and usually if they get enough rope they hang themselves.'

I hoped that would happen soon.

*

I met Doro outside the store one afternoon. I'd seen her from a distance a few times and was looking forward to talking to her, hoping she'd be my kind of person. I was loving getting to know the Indigenous folk of Mount Allan and living and working amongst them but I needed some of my own kind too. Doro worked in the community art centre. She was a big built woman with a strong German accent. Her constant companion was a Great Dane called Pascha, who either trotted faithfully along beside her or lay sprawled and panting, waiting for their next move.

'I just have to go back to the art centre to finish up,' Doro told me in her straightforward, no-nonsense way, 'then we can go back to my house for a drink. Come. Let me show you.'

Unceremonious as the corrugated-iron art centre appeared from the outside, inside was a different story. The walls were adorned with paintings that featured the intricate symbols and dots of Central Australian Aboriginal art. The paintings were done on canvas fabric then stretched and mounted onto wooden frames. Doro showed me the process. There were framed paintings leaning against the walls too and then a whole lot of unframed canvases in piles on some tables near the door. On other tables were wooden artefacts: boomerangs and other hand-carved implements of various shapes and sizes, many of which had been painted and decorated.

'We catalogue and display all this,' Doro told me, 'and promote it. Isn't it wonderful? Mount Allan art is highly regarded in Australia and overseas.'

'Who's we?' I asked, looking from Doro to the dog.

'No, not Pascha,' she laughed. 'But you would if you could wouldn't you, Pascha?'

Pascha, sprawled out on the floor and panting, looked up at her with his big, doggy eyes as if to say indeed he would if only he had the energy.

Doro laughed good-naturedly and continued. 'Bob and I,' she said. 'He's the other art coordinator. He's away a lot, doing the promotion and selling. We're having an exhibition in Sydney early next year and he's working on one in Berlin.'

From this corrugated-iron shed to the shining galleries of the world's great cities. I wondered if the fancy folk who admired these art works and put them on display in their galleries and living rooms had any concept of where they came from and the conditions under which they were produced.

At various places across the paint-spattered concrete floor were unfinished canvases surrounded by jars of paint.

'Some artists like to come in here and paint,' Doro told me, 'away from the heat and flies. Then they can just leave their work spread out overnight and it will be safe here.'

'Do you have any of Maureen's paintings?' I asked her, looking around hopefully.

'Maureen Hudson? No. I think she has her own dealers in town. Some artists choose to sell their work directly to the galleries in town.' She shrugged and made a face like she was a bit put out. 'They sometimes pay more but they can rip the artists off too. It just depends. Community art centres like this one protect the artists and involve them in the marketing and selling of their work. But Maureen's doing well on her own, making a name for herself.'

Doro had been fiddling around while we talked but I hadn't been paying much attention. I'd been following her around, admiring the smorgasbord of art and intrigued by this aspect of life at Mount Allan. Now she had switched off the lights and was opening the tin shed door.

'Come on. Would you like to come back to my place?' she invited.

'Yes, but I'd also like to go for a walk. I feel like I need some exercise.'

Doro nodded emphatically.

'Would you like to come?' I asked her.

'I would love to but it's still a bit hot. Come back home and have a drink and we can go for a walk in an hour.'

I trotted along, pleased to have a new friend.

'We can walk out that way,' Doro told me, pointing east to a rocky mountain range in the distance. I've asked.'

'Are there places we can't walk?' I asked innocently.

'Of course,' she snapped. 'There are sacred sites that people don't want us walking on. We mustn't go walking anywhere around here without getting permission.'

I felt chastised and there was an awkward silence then Doro spoke again more gently. 'I talk to people about sacred sites and dreaming stories all day. That's what they are painting.'

A group of kids was flocking our way, chattering like a bunch of finches.

'Miss Kumenjayi.'

'Doro.'

'Allo, Doro.'

'Germany Dog, Germany Dog.'

Some of them started patting Pascha and one tried to mount him like a horse amidst giggles from the crowd. Doro gently but firmly protected Pascha and showed the kids how to treat him kindly.

'Where you going, Miss Kumenjayi?'

'Where you going, Doro?'

'We're going to Doro's house.'

'Can we come?'

'Can we come?'

'Can we come?'

It was like the line of a song they were singing in chorus.

'No, not this time,' Doro replied and I was pleased. Sometimes we needed time out.

Doro lived in a little demountable house at ground level. It was less of a caravan than my place but still tinny and flimsy. Once inside, she led the way down a narrow corridor to the living area. It was dark and cool, simply and comfortably furnished and, overall, a welcome retreat.

Perhaps the most striking feature of Doro's home were the magnificent paintings that adorned her walls. It was the art she worked with: age-old Dreaming stories that derived from local lands, told through the iconography of Central Australia then completed with decorative dots and brushstrokes, all in earthy desert tones.

'It's one way I can support the artists.' Doro shrugged her trademark dismissive shrug like nothing was too much of a big deal or too much bother. 'I can't help myself,' she laughed. 'I just love them. Anyway, what else am I going to spend my money on out here?'

We waited until late afternoon then headed west; past a large river red gum that stood like a sentinel where the community finished and the wilderness began. Bushes and grasses dominated the plains and little delights abounded: a shrub adorned with delicate flowers; a small plant bearing deep purple berries; patches of bare earth that bore the imprints of small creatures. Birds chattered and darted in crazy flocks from one bush to the next. It was cooler now in the late afternoon and a refreshing breeze blew across the land, caressing us and whispering in the bushes.

I loved being out in that country; the sense of timelessness, the peaceful solitude. Living out in the desert held a mystery for me, a magic, that I felt every day I was there. That was amplified when I left the community and stepped out into the bush.

We followed a track that led us to the rocky ranges we saw in the distance from Mount Allan. It was cooler there, and damp. Different plants grew in and around the ranges: little ferns and palm trees and plants with shiny, dark green leaves. It felt more familiar to me, like places where I had grown up.

We found some gently sloping rock with ledges that formed natural seats. The rock was cool and smooth to touch as we sat to take in the world around us. A gentle breeze whispered through the bushes, in the distance a flock of birds darted as one from one bush to the next. A lizard scurried along the ground and popped down a hole. Don't worry, lizard, we're out-of-towners and not the hunting kind. And then there were the perpetual pesky flies.

Apart from those flashes of movement, the land seemed strikingly still. Like if you looked down and looked up again quickly it would all be just the same. Like if you closed your eyes for ten thousand years then opened them again, nothing would have changed. The hot dry open conditions weren't conducive to the processes of life at the speed they happened in the forests of the south. Death. Decomposition. New life. Growth. Things happened slowly out there.

It wasn't just one mountain range we'd come to but an area of hills and gullies. We went from ridges down into the valleys and wandered apart to explore on our own, trees full of strange fruits, pretty scented grasses that seemed to grow out of sheer rock. Then we'd cooee out to each other and come together again, to keep in touch and share what we had found.

Stumbling down one rocky slope, I startled a rock wallaby, or was it a rock wallaby that startled me? I jumped as it turned and hopped away, sure-footed even in this rough terrain.

We walked back home as the sun was setting, oohing and ahhing at the colours in the sky. A gathering of clouds to the west seemed to somehow reflect the fading sun. Those clouds boasted the prettiest shade of pink to red and then maroon, growing deeper as the night moved in. Some sunsets were surprisingly gentle, just a soft golden glow that faded into night. Cloud in the western sky, as on this occasion, resulted in a brilliant evening performance of pattern and colour.

'Come over for a dinner and a drink one night,' Doro invited at the crossroads, back in the community, where she went one way and I another.

'What kind of a drink?' I asked.

Doro shrugged. 'You'll have to wait and see.'

I wandered home beneath the Milky Way, pleased that I had a new friend.

*

On Monday of week two, Alison sidled up to me in the school ground at recess and gently stroked my arm. 'Miss Kumenjayi,' she murmured. At upper primary school age, Alison was one of our senior pupils, and a regular attender. She lived with her father and three older brothers in a house across from mine. She was well dressed and seemed cared for but she conveyed a soft longing, perhaps because her mother had died a while back. Alison stood close to me while the other kids arrived.

Loretta and Blackie walked up holding hands.

'Miss Kumenjayi,' Loretta announced.

'Yes, Loretta.'

'Um,' like she had just said my name for the sake of it and had nothing to follow up with, 'dis my sister. Dis Blackie.'

Blackie, at five, was one of our youngest. She was a smaller, less tamed version of Loretta and as cute as a baby bilby. Blackie looked up at me with her big brown eyes and giggled.

'Yeah, I know Blackie. Hello, Blackie.'

'Allo,' she replied boldly.

Loretta and Blackie nestled in close while we waited for the others to arrive, back from their morning break.

A group came belting up, almost knocking us flying in their enthusiasm to reach us first. As they tagged me they called out, 'First.' 'Second.' 'Third.' And so on, until they ran out of names for the ordinals.

One of the racers was Andrew. '*Ngurrdju mayi?*' he asked, looking up into my face and trying to catch his breath. Andrew was the same age as Alison and another regular attender.

The assembled group was looking at me, waiting for my response to Andrew's question.

I shrugged. I didn't understand.

'*Ngurrdju*,' he repeated. 'You know it?'

I shook my head and replied, '*Lawa*. No.'

'You gotta say *Ngurrdju mayi*. It means like this, Are you good?'

'*Nor-joo mayi*,' I attempted.

'Nah, *ngurrdju*,' he tried again, slowly and carefully enunciating the first word for me while all the others looked on hopefully.

'*Nor-joo*,' I said again but I knew I wasn't getting it right.

'Nah, you gotta say *Ngurrdju. Ngu. Ngu*,' patiently making the sound at the start of the word where I was getting it wrong. It started with the 'ng' sound like English has at the end of words like running and skipping and jumping. It's hard for me to make that sound at the start of the word, particularly when it's followed by a rolled 'rr'. It seems my tongue wasn't designed to work that way.

Other kids joined in, saying it en masse as if all of them talking at once would help. I tried to study the way they were holding their mouths and imitate as best I could. My young teachers kept shaking their heads and carefully repeating the word until they were either satisfied with my pronunciation or gave up in frustration.

In this way, on many occasions, they taught me several words and phrases from their languages, Warlpiri and Anmatyerre. I knew some

German and Italian but the Aboriginal languages were entirely different; bearing no resemblance to the European ones whatsoever. I listened to kids talking away in their languages and wondered whether this rapid-fire communication was really language with grammar and order that I could ever get my head around, let alone my tongue.

The kids experienced similar difficulties with English pronunciation.

One day Loretta was reading me a story that featured a buffalo. 'Buppalo,' is how she said it.

'Say buffalo,' I told her.

'Buppalo,' she replied.

I broke it down for her. 'Say buff.'

'Buff,' she said.

'Say alo.'

'Alo,' she said.

'Now say buffalo.'

She took a deep breath, screwed up her face and tried with all her might. 'Fuffalo,' is what came out.

It seemed like a simple arrangement of sounds to me, just as *ngurrdju* seemed easy to them.

4

There were just six weeks of the school year left when I started teaching at Mount Allan. I was replacing a popular young man who had met a tragic end. One weekend while riding his motorbike on a dirt road way out bush, he ran into a patch of bulldust on the side of the road and lost control. By the time someone came across him, he was dead. Enough time had passed since his death for the community to be ready for a replacement.

The people of Mount Allan never mentioned him to me. It was as if he had never existed. That's how it was out there. Once a person died, they were never mentioned again, to allow their spirit to go free.

My life took on a regular rhythm. There was the penetrating heat, the radiant light, the vast open space of each new day dawning in the desert.

I walked to school: across the cul-de-sac, between the store and the art gallery, over the rocks, up the hill, down the other side and through the hotch-potch grid of roads and tracks and people's accommodation. I loved my walk to school through the community with the desert wilderness as a backdrop. I sometimes thought about my city peers with their commute down congested streets and I felt glad to be where I was.

In yards, small breakfast fires were flickering, even at this hot time of year. People were slowly stirring, emerging from their homes or their swags on the ground.

At eight in the morning, it was already bright and hot. During the long, hot summer, that went for at least half the year, the sun rose at about five and the temperature climbed steadily from that time on. Even early in the morning, the intensity of the sun could burn my fair skin and render me slow and casual. The sky was usually perfect blue contrasted against the burnt-orange earth.

There were dogs slinking around as usual: skinny, naked things. One stopped on the track in front of me, to point its bony arse down and squeeze out a turd that would dry quickly in the penetrating sun. The dogs seemed sulky and obedient to their masters but I'm sure they knew I didn't approve of them with their scattered turds and mangy bodies and that's why they looked at me slyly and stopped in front of me to do their business.

Smells wafted through the air: the refuse of poorly sanitised human settlement, freshly squeezed dog shit, breakfast cooking.

'Goot morning,' from the first camp I walked past. I wasn't sure who it was but it didn't really matter. I had the feeling we were all in this together.

'Morning,' I called back.

'Goot morning, Miss Kumenjayi,' from an early riser coming towards me on the track. It was Sandy Allan, chirpy and buoyant.

'Morning, Sandy. Are you well?'

'*Yuwayi*,' he boomed out. '*Kele nyuntu*? Yes. How about you?'

'*Ngurrdju*,' I replied, saying that damned word as best I could.

Sandy laughed. People tended to laugh good-naturedly at my mispronunciations whereas I never laughed at theirs.

'How much your car, Miss Kumenjayi?'

'A million dollars.'

'*Nyuru*, okay,' and he laughed again. 'You hab a good day, Miss Kumenjayi.'

'You too, Sandy.'

'Morning,' from one camp.

'Morning,' from another.

'Morning.'

It was like the morning song, I mused, a flock of humans singing in the new day.

I replied and sometimes managed words in my limited Warlpiri or Anmatyerre.

'*Ngurrdju mayi*? Are you well?'

'*Yuwayi, kele nyuntu*? Yes, how about you?'

'*Ngaka nyanku nyanyi*. See you later.'

People laughed and responded in strings of rapid language which they knew were all too much for me.

Kids waved from their yards and called out my name. 'There's Kumenjayi,' I could hear them saying to their adults, with the proud ownership that kids feel for their schoolteachers.

That was one way I got in with the adults, through caring for their kids.

Loretta and Blackie skipped up beside me and slipped their hands into mine, one on either side.

'Miss Kumenjayi.'

'Loretta.'

'Miss Kumenjayi.'

'Blackie.'

We laughed and sang and swang our arms, all the way to school.

Alastair's Land Rover was out the front so I sent the kids off to brush their teeth and went in for our morning talk. He was sitting at his desk with a cup of tea attending to paperwork.

'Morning,' he bellowed out in his slightly amused, sergeant major way. He enquired briefly into my health but almost before I could answer, off he went with his rave: ideas and plans for the coming day, community news, complaints about the difficult conditions under which we worked, sad stories about the backgrounds and poor health of our pupils.

Alastair did most of the talking. I listened and took it all in, sifting through the information he offered and making my own assessments. He was married to a local woman and had a wealth of experience living in these parts. I valued the knowledge he readily shared but sometimes I felt at odds with the way he saw things and was developing perspectives of my own.

We were interrupted by little voices at the open door.

'Jakamarra.'

'Morning, Loretta. Morning, Blackie.'

'We wanna come in.'

'Not school time yet,' he told them. 'Here.' He produced a ball from under his desk.

Loretta ran over and grabbed it keenly then disappeared back outside.

'Why do they call you Jakamarra?' I asked.

'That's my skin name. Alastair is Kumenjayi too so they won't say that. I'm Jakamarra because I'm married to Ada.'

'What's she?'

'She's Napaljari.'

'Right,' I said in a way that suggested that I didn't understand at all.

Alastair went on to give me my first lesson about skin names. 'Everyone has a skin name,' he told me. 'They're born into it, depending on what their parents' skin names are. I'm Jakamarra. My wife is Napaljarri, so we're right skin. Jakamarra and Napaljarri are meant to marry. Our girls are automatically Napurrulas. If we had any boys, they would be Jupurrula. See, the girls all start with N and the boys with J.'

'How many skin names are there?' I asked.

'Eight.'

'And who are your girls meant to marry?'

'Napurrula marries Japanangka.'

'And does Jupurrula marry Napanangka?' I asked uncertainly, stumbling over the words and the concepts.

'That's right, you've got it,' he replied happily. 'And their kids will be Japangardi if they're boys…'

'And Napangardi if they're girls,' I interjected.

'Well done,' he replied.

'What if people want to marry someone who hasn't got the right skin for them?' I asked.

'Big trouble,' Alastair replied, shaking his head. 'Mostly they don't. Only in towns, away from the watchful eye of the community and where there's grog involved. In the past, if wrong skin people got together, they were punished severely.'

'Like how?' I asked.

Alastair shrugged. 'There are stories of wrong skin couples who were banished from their communities.'

'Forever?' I asked.

'Yep, forever. Otherwise people might be speared, maybe killed.'

'Wow, that's harsh.'

Alastair nodded. 'That's how these societies survived, for tens of thousands of years. They were disciplined. There was the law and mostly people followed it without question. Anyone who did the wrong thing was punished harshly.'

'What did skin names have to do with survival?' I asked.

'The skin system is a complicated mathematical structure that prevents inbreeding. You have to remember the genetic pool out here was quite small so you couldn't have people breeding with their closest relatives. But it's about more than that,' he continued. 'Skin names let everyone know how they're related to everyone else in a place where relationships are all-important. Don't worry,' he reassured me. 'It will make sense eventfully and you'll be given a skin name of your own.'

I looked forward to getting a skin name that I interpreted as an indication of a deeper level of acceptance.

It was ten o'clock by then, way after school was meant to start.

Alastair jumped up all of a sudden like he'd just been bitten on the arse by a redback spider and announced, 'We must ring the bell.'

It was a real bell that hung just outside the door, the kind you get on Christmas cards. It had a chain hanging down from the centre that you shook back and forth to make the sound.

The clang clang clang brought the kids, skipping and running, into the grounds where we met them. Some were clean and bright, smelling of soap and shampoo; wet, dark curls slicked down in an attempt to tame that which would spring and knot back up during the course of the day. Others were dusty and dishevelled, like they'd just rolled out of bed, often wearing the same clothes they'd had on for days. Some kids raced in, first to the teacher. From quite a distance out, I saw them take off running, then burn in through the gate, charging over to me and grabbing me or tapping me as they arrived.

First.

Second.

Third.

And so on.

Others meandered in, shirtless, shoeless, hair all over the place. Most arrived with big, shy grins.

'Morning, Kumenjayi. Morning, Jakamarra,' they yelled out then scampered off to the ablutions block for teeth cleaning and face washing. They were well established rituals that the kids seemed to embrace: their own brush, the wriggly white toothpaste worms and the fresh mint taste. They liked to splash water over their faces, wash away the sleep and the snot and freshen up.

Younger kids and those who didn't attend school as regularly hid behind those who were more confident. They held hands, walked arm in arm, were physical and affectionate with each other. They stuck together, supporting and interpreting for each other in the strange school environment.

Maureen sauntered in with Gwenda and Anderson. They were calm and groomed. Other mornings, Maureen arrived with eight children, sometimes with the entire school population for the day.

*

Eventually, after everyone had cleaned themselves up, had a game and a giggle, the odd fight, a few tears shed or a public sulk, it was time for an organised ball game and then inside. The kids raced to the bottom of the stairs and lined up in proper colonial style. It was part of the game of school that they seemed to know and like.

On cue, the children marched up the stairs and into the classroom. As they passed through the doorway, Alastair waved his hands in front of and behind each child, like a ritual blessing. It was actually a practical gesture to remove the clouds of flies that were attached to each child before they were brought into the room.

They yelled and fought over seats and pencil cases, scrambled for tissues, talked and laughed and raised general chaos for a short amount of time. There was no point in trying to control it. Suddenly everyone was seated and finally content with their arrangement. They were quiet and still, facing the front, no fiddling.

Samuel had his head down and was muttering into the desk. He was eight years old, hard of hearing and often out of sorts with the world. Kids often got upset and were quite expressive about it. Mostly they did a bit of cursing, made out like they were going to hit someone and then they settled down. Every now and again, like Samuel now, an aggrieved kid would end up face down on the desk, arms above their heads, immutable. Nothing could move them: not humour nor threats nor gentle teasing, nor care, nothing, until they were ready.

Suddenly Samuel rose and pushed his chair back, where it teetered unsteadily before tipping over. He then raised his hand as if he was going to slam it down on the head of the boy sitting next to him before pouncing out the door and down the stairs.

'Let him go,' said Alastair. 'He'll be back when he feels better.'

I stood at the door and watched as Samuel flounced out the school gate and back to his house, two doors up.

*

'Good morning, Mount Allan School.'

'Goot morning, Alastair. Goot morning, Miss Kumenjayi. Goot morning, Maureen,' in that droning way that schoolkids have of talking en masse.

Roll call came next. Alastair usually did that in his mock sergeant major way.

'Janie.'

'Here.'

'Andrew Barnes.'

'Here.'

'Joey.'

'Here.'

'Big bird.'

'Here.'

(Plenty of kids' names were Kumenjayi and they went by an assortment of nicknames and local, bush names.)

'Kinyariya.'

'No. She's town. She's town.'

'Felicity.'

'Sleep.'

'Oh, she's asleep, is she? Late night?' There was no response so he continued. 'Marshall.'

Marshall was small and cute and new to school processes.

'Marshall,' Alastair repeated in a fun way, looking at Marshall.

Still there was no response.

'Marshall,' he repeated again, stringing the name out, looking directly at Marshall.

''Ere,' Marshall finally managed, giggling so sweetly that the rest of us giggled along with him.

'Gracie.'

'Here.' Barely audible. Shy little Gracie.

Alastair stopped and looked up. 'Oh, you're here today?' smiling kindly.

Gracie smiled back timidly and nodded.

'Good girl,' he told her. 'We're happy to see you at school.'

Gracie's smile turned into a beam then she put her head down, embarrassed.

'Banjo.'

'Puneral, Yuendumu.'

'Oh, he's gone to Yuendumu. Who else has gone to that funeral?'

The kids looked around and started calling out names.

Roll call was a way of recording attendance, welcoming students individually, modelling the English language and sharing community information.

Next came singing, in English and in Warlpiri. The Warlpiri language had received far more attention from linguists and teachers across the area than had Anmatyerre. Many songs and storybooks had been written and recorded in Warlpiri. When we wanted to incorporate the children's own language into the school program, using the resources that were available, it was much easier to do that with Warlpiri. This was despite the fact that half of the kids on the community came from backgrounds where Anmatyerre was the first language.

Alastair led the singing, modelling himself on some distinguished conductor. He had the words of the regular school songs written up on big sheets of butcher's paper for everyone to follow. He pointed to each word with the long blackboard ruler as we went,

> This land is your land
> This land is my land
> From California
> To the New York Island
> From the redwood forest
> To the Gulf Stream waters
> This land was made for you and me
>
> As I was walking a ribbon of highway
> I saw above me an endless skyway
> I saw below me a golden valley
> this land was made for you and me

After a while, we rewrote the lyrics with the students to localise the song and give it new meaning:

> This land is your land
> This land is my land
> From Kumenjayi Springs
> To Yuelamu
> From the rocky ranges
> To the sandy rivers
> This land was made for you and me
>
> As I was walking on the Tanami Highway
> I saw above me an endless skyway

> I saw below me the hot red sand
> This land was made for you and me

After singing came storytelling on the mat. The kids all sat up cross-legged with their backs straight and arms folded across their chests. The teachers sat on chairs up the front.

I directed the storytelling. 'Who's first?'

'Big bird.'

'Nah, Joey.'

'Nah, Mildred. Mildred.'

They dobbed each other in until someone was prepared to get the ball rolling.

'Yeserday I went to dam,' announced Mildred.

'Thanks, Mildred,' I replied. 'What did you do at the dam?'

'We was swimming. And we saw ducks.'

'Were there ducks at the dam yesterday?'

Mildred nodded happily.

A whole lot of kids were flapping their arms in the air by now and trying to sit up the straightest so they would be picked, eyes bulging with enthusiasm.

'Yes, David.'

Groans of displeasure at not being picked and all the hands went down.

'Yesterday we came back from Willowra.'

'Why did you go to Willowra?' I asked.

'Pamily. To see pamily.'

'Did you have a good time?'

David nodded keenly.

'What time did you come home?'

He looked perplexed, trying to find the right word. '*Uradji*,' he finally said.

'Was it dark?' I asked.

A few kids started to call out.

'I'm just asking David,' I told them. 'Was it dark, David?'

He shrugged then replied, 'Little bit.'

'Thanks, David. Who's next?'

'Me, me.' Pulka was waving his hand so frantically I thought he might burst.

'Yes, Pulka.'

His big grin was infectious. There was a pause while he assembled his thoughts and perhaps figured out how to get them out of his mouth in English. He'd been so keen to have a turn but now that it had finally arrived, he was struggling. When he finally spoke, the words came pouring out in one long line. 'Yesterday we went to town and then we came back and my uncles was drinking and fighting and when we came back I saw Miss Kumenjayi.'

It must have been a combination of the content, his awkwardness, the speed of delivery and his big grin, but the whole assembled mass of kids fell about laughing, Pulka included.

I let them go for a while, laughing and exclaiming in their languages, then I crossed my arms over my chest. Someone took my cue and did the same, sitting up straight and facing the front. Others followed and soon everyone was back, in order and composed.

'What did you do in town, Pulka?'

He shrugged. 'Hot chips.'

'Oh, you had hot chips. Anything else?'

He nodded. 'Shop,' he said.

'You went to the shop. Which shop.'

'Kmart.'

'Oh, you went to Kmart. What did you get?'

'Clothes,' he replied and I realised he was wearing them, jeans and a nice new shirt.'

'They look really nice, Pulka. Well done,' I told him.

Pulka sat up straight then, looking very pleased with himself.

Gracie sat up the back, thin and waiflike, with straggly, sun-bleached hair and a soft, reserved demeanour. She hardly ever came to school. Her family travelled between communities, Maureen had told me, and spent time at each of them. Gracie was enrolled in several schools but attended none of them very frequently.

During a lull in the high energy proceedings, I looked at Gracie and asked her, 'Gracie, what's your story?'

The kids all sat quietly to give her a go. Waiting.

Maureen spoke to her in Warlpiri, inviting her to speak.

Gracie nodded barely perceptibly.

I looked at Maureen, who nodded at me. I then looked back to Gracie and smiled.

When she was ready, she spoke in little more than a whisper. 'Yesterday we bin come back to Warriyi Warriyi.'

'Yeterday you came back to where?'

She took a moment. 'Warriyi Warriyi,' she whispered again.

'Mount Allan,' the kids were calling out in unison, 'Mount Allan.'

I looked to Maureen for clarification.

'*Yuwayi*,' Maureen said. 'Warriyi Warriyi is name for Mount Allan.'

'Where does it come from?'

'Warriyi Warriyi is that little bush you see everywhere round here. It's bush medicine plant. We boil up the leaves for sores.'

'And that's what you call Mount Allan?'

'Bush name, bush name,' some of the kids were saying. 'Warriyi Warriyi, Miss Kumenjayi. You gotta call it Warriyi Warriyi.'

From then on, it was the name I preferred and I realised it was how the people of this place generally referred to their community. Mount Allan was the whitefella name, used initially for the cattle station. Yuelamu was like the official Aboriginal name, actually derived from an area to the west of the community. The most grassroots, least political of the names was Warriyi Warriyi. The place, like each person, had several names, each with its own connotations.

After the children had told their stories, they went back to their desks to record them in their writing books. The most advanced students wrote independently, using junior dictionaries and the word banks displayed around the walls. Others laboured to produce a few words. Some students told their stories through illustrations which they then explained to one or other of the teachers. We summed up their story in a sentence or two then wrote it on a piece of paper for them to copy into their book or dotted it onto their page for them to trace over.

In the daily writing session, there were activities to suit each student, at their level of development. One of the challenges of our multilevel classroom was to provide educational activities appropriate for students at all their different ages and levels of ability.

When the older, more advanced students had finished their work, they went and helped younger family members, often by completing their work for them. When I first saw this, my inclination was to tell them off. Helping was one thing but doing someone else's work for them got in the way of them developing their own skills. Then I realised that helping was so intrinsically part of those bush children's way: sharing and caring and taking responsibility for younger family members. To reprimand them for doing what was such an intrinsic and appealing part of who those kids were seemed unnecessary and counter-productive.

As Shimpo wrote,

> The teacher raises a question such as, 'What is the answer to 7 x 7?' Students tend to be contented if anyone, possibly the bright one, knows the answer, because the student will be regarded as the temporary leader of their group. Whereas in the modern school system, teachers expect every one of their students to learn the subject. The two sets of expectations conflict in the school…

Another challenge seemed to be in finding ways to teach the bush kids what they needed to know in the modern school system but incorporate or allow enough of their ways into the program that school didn't feel alien or hostile. Having local community people involved in the kid's education was a key to its success. I wondered, was this the two-way schooling Kevin Buzzacott talked about?

The students took delight in illustrating their stories; often complex, detailed drawings done in the styles of the two worlds in which they lived: the traditional symbols of Central Australian art, combined with more still life representations: *yapa* and *kardiya* interpretations of life expressed through the children's art.

When everyone was finished, the author or one of the teachers read the stories to the class and held up the pictures. The kids sat up attentively during this activity and laughed good-naturedly at each other's drawings.

This morning session finished at smoko time and the kids nicked off home for half an hour.

*

After school one afternoon, Maureen took me to the dam. As we walked, she slipped her hand into mine and quietly said, 'You're Nampijinpa, my sister.'

My heart skipped a beat with this next step in acceptance and belonging.

As we strolled, children joined us from all directions. Maureen introduced me to any children I hadn't met: visitors from neighbouring communities and the ones who came and went. The children chattered and laughed all around us. Sometimes I felt a little hand slip into mine and we walked along like that, holding hands and swinging arms. Just as suddenly, the hand slipped out again and merged in with the crowd.

The closer we came to the dam, the more green and lush the environment became. It was about a kilometre across and held a lot more water than I'd expected to see in the Tanami Desert. The dam was set in a gentle, natural valley and surrounded by ghost gums and grass. A different feeling existed here, a particular life force that comes with water. It was like a piece of my southern country.

Dead trees stood, black and contorted, deep in the water. The branches of those trees were lined with some indecipherable mass. This turned into pelicans as we approached, which rose up then flocked down to the water to paddle around, searching for food. There were also ducks, black swans, herons and other long-legged, long-necked waterbirds.

The kids who'd been lingering along, running here and there, took off ahead as we approached the water. They stripped off to underwear or shorts, tossing their clothes to the ground as they went and, keeping up the momentum, dived straight in. Then they surfaced, like crazy brown ducks, to call out, 'Maureen, watch me, watch me. Kumenjayi, look me.'

They flipped upside down to stand on their hands, do somersaults, duck dive. They climbed onto branches and swung from the rope, back and forward, back and forward then, whoosh, into the water. The kids took care of each other, with the older ones in particular looking out for the littlies. I resisted impulses to rant and rave and assume teacherly control. Instead I followed Maureen's lead. She seemed to trust their abilities and let them be. We talked and laughed at their antics as the sun dropped lower and began to cast a golden glow over the water and surrounding land.

'I'd like to walk around the dam,' I announced innocently.

One of the older girls gasped. 'No, you can't,' she told me in a low, deep growl. '*Kadaicha.*'

'Yes, *kadaicha* might come,' Maureen agreed quietly.

We assembled and strolled back. Along the way I asked them about this *kadaicha*. At the very mention of the name, some seizure took hold of the group and the conversation dropped in tone and volume.

'You gotta look out. He comes at night.'

'He got emu-feather boots.'

'He can make your tyres flat or murder you.'

'He fly sometime. He move really fast.'

The children were dramatic. Their voices were low and quiet to display the awe and fear they held for *kadaicha* man. I laughed at their earnestness.

'No, not funny,' one girl growled at me.

'True God, isn't it, Maureen?'

'*Yuwayi,*' she whispered.

The most serious things were whispered.

I visited the dam often then, in the afternoon but well before dark. I would swim into the middle and back, striding it out like I used to do in the ocean and public swimming pools, for exercise and well-being. It came as welcome relief in a place where exercise was hard to come by; because it was often too hot, I was often quite tired and exercise wasn't a priority for just about anyone who lived anywhere near me.

5

For a few days each week, I was a schoolteacher at Mount Allan, supporting Alastair and Maureen. On the other days, I worked at Pulardi as the visiting outstation teacher. To get there, I drove sixty kilometres along the main road, back towards Alice Springs. At the car bonnet sign on the side of the road, I turned left onto a narrow track that took me through the bush to the little homeland settlement.

Teddy Briscoe was the head man and he lived there with his wife, four grown-up sons and daughters and their partners and children. Everyone came and went a bit, to the nearby communities of Mount Allan and Laramba or into Alice Springs. A core group generally stayed in one place but I never knew from one visit to the next who would be at Pulardi when I arrived and which kids would turn up for school.

I pulled up at the school building and my four main charges came bounding over from their house. It was one of eight at this settlement, set casually around a central square that was well shaded by some large, established cedar trees. On the outskirts of this little village were a windmill and pump, a vegetable garden and a fenced yard containing horses. Pulardi outstation felt organised and well cared for.

'Miss Kumenjayi.'

'Miss Kumenjayi.'

'Miss Kumenjayi.'

'Miss Kumenjayi.'

Hugs, salutations, snot inadvertently transferred to my clothes. I was used to that by now. I wore my clothes for several days in a row, like the people I lived amongst, and relished the code of the bush: crumpled, stained and comfortable.

'You look like proper bush woman now,' Brenda had laughed at me recently and I took that as some kind of compliment.

Brenda was Teddy's daughter-in-law and the mother of Cameron, Alvin, Katrina and Stephanie, the four who had bowled over to greet me. They made up half the school population of Pulardi and were my most regular attendees.

The kids clambered around the school door and went flooding in as I pushed it open. The schoolroom was exactly the same as when I'd left it last week, untouched in my absence. It wasn't possible to lock Pulardi Outstation School but no one ever went into it unless the teacher was there and school was on. No one would dare. Teddy Briscoe held a reverence for education that he passed on to the rest of his family.

'Lego, Lego, we wanna play Lego.'

They waited until I gave the nod, same procedure every time, then dived on the box of Lego and emptied it onto the floor. They then busied themselves with construction as though their lives depended on it, chatting away as they went.

The school was one large room with a blackboard mounted on the wall at the far end. Behind that was a cordoned-off storage area. One of the long central walls could be slid back to open up that whole side of the building and allow in light and air. It also let the desert in; a beautiful living landscape. There were moments, with the wall slid back and the students absorbed in their activities, that I breathed in that desertscape and felt I had the sanest job in the sanest place on earth.

Brenda turned up with little Maxie trotting along behind her. He fitted into the extended family, although I was never quite sure how. Maxie was three, so officially too young for school and too young to go on the roll. He was generally naked with his hair sticking out all over the place, a string of green snot dripping from his nose and joy written all over his dear little face.

'Maxie,' I exclaimed and he grinned up at me.

Brenda and I laughed. She cleaned his face and he sat down with the big kids to join in with the Lego. How could we turn away such enthusiasm and cuteness? Maxie had an attention span commensurate with his age so he played for a while then wandered back to the adults in the community, leaving us to get on with our schoolwork.

The program we taught was based on workbooks designed for this kind of school setting. They contained literacy and numeracy activities for the students to work at their own pace, with assistance as required. We established a routine that also included other school activities such as songs, stories, sport and art. The theory was that Brenda, who was employed as the assistant teacher, could continue running that program on the days that I wasn't there.

There was a song we sang often that became one of our favourites. I think the kids enjoyed the cultural recognition and a smattering of words from their own language. It had a catchy tune too.

> Ah we
> Are the children of the bush
> We walk through the seasons
> As they change around us
> And we like to gather bush tucker
> When we put it in our tummies
> It makes us feel good
>
> I like to munch on *parla, parla, parla*
> I like to munch on *parla*
> It grows on a vine in the trees.

There were several verses that went through Indigenous bush foods, calling them by their local names.

At morning tea time while the rest of the kids wandered back to their camp, Alvin stayed behind to work on his Lego construction. He was five years of age. His hair was cut spiky short, due to the head lice that constantly plagued those kids. He was dressed in shorts and a crumpled T-shirt that he'd been wearing for days. His feet were bare and carried the scars of sores on the mend. His skin was brown and dusty. Alvin was completely immersed in what he was building and oblivious to anything else.

As I sat on a school table watching Alvin, I was overwhelmed by his childish attention to detail, his absorption in the moment, the way he was building a Lego wall as if the whole future of civilisation depended on it. I loved what I knew of Alvin too: his ready laughter, his stoicism and his freedom in the bush.

I adored all the kids I worked with out there but at that moment it was embodied in Alvin. I wondered if I would have as much love for anyone ever again as I did for him right then.

He looked up at me and grinned shyly then went back to his construction.

Brenda wandered back after a while, Maxie in tow. 'Schooltime?' she asked me.

'Yep, schooltime.'

'You gotta call the kids. Say *kweremup pitchey*.'

'*Kweremup pitchey*,' I replied, trying to sound as much like her as possible.

'*Yuwayi, kwereempu pitchey*. In Anmatyerre it means, Kids come here.'

I took a breath and yelled out across the camp, '*Kweremup pitchey*,' the way I had seen people do so often, attempting to imitate their intonation.

I heard people laugh and the kids came running, big grins across their faces. They loved it when whitefellas had a go at speaking their language and responded more readily than if I had called out the English equivalent.

'You're talking Anmatyerre now, Miss Kumenjayi,' Cameron told me happily. 'You're talking our language.'

I wished I could manage more than a few simple phrases.

After school, Teddy called me over. He tended to hold court in the central meeting place, his swag for a throne, upon which he sat cross-legged like an outback Budda. Teddy's voice boomed out, laughing or growling, which he did in equal measure.

Teddy had been the head stockman at nearby Napperby Station for sixteen years, at a time when Aboriginal people were the backbone of the Central Australian cattle industry and paid in rations. He was a confident man and strong in his culture but he also embraced the ways of white people.

'You kids gotta learn,' he growled at his grandchildren if he so much as sniffed any dissent towards school. In a place where many of the adults seemed ambivalent towards Whitefella education, Teddy's attitude was heartening and gave meaning to my job.

Teddy was a Jampijinba. As a Nampijinpa, I was his sister.

'Come over here, Nampijinpa,' he hollered. He patted the swag and invited me to sit down beside him. '*Marre*? Are you good?' he asked in Anmatyerre.

'*Marre anthurre*. I am very good,' I replied proudly.

Teddy laughed out loud at my apparent confidence in getting my tongue around his language. *Marre anthurre* and now *kweremup pitchey* were about as far as I went. I could listen to people speaking Anmatyerre and sometimes get the gist of what they were saying but in general my language learning was frustratingly limited. Nevertheless, people seemed pleased at my attempts.

'You happy at Pulardi.'

'I love it out here ,Teddy,' I told him. 'I love the kids and being out here in the bush and getting to know you people.'

'And the kids are right at school? They doing their work?'

I grinned. 'The kids are great. They're doing very well. You have very good grandchildren.'

Teddy nodded and smiled warmly. 'Where your family?' he asked me.

I told him about my parents, down in suburban Melbourne.

He shook his head. 'Long way, too far.'

'Yeah,' I shrugged. 'They write me letters and I go and see them when I can. They're coming to visit too. I get a bit lonely sometimes but it's okay. I'm happy to be here.'

Teddy nodded and thought about that. 'We might get you husband,' he offered.

'Do you think it's all right for black people and white people to go together?' I asked.

'Course it's all right if they love each other. We might have different colour skin,' he told me, 'but we all got the same blood.'

*

Eventually someone showed me the back way to and from Mount Allan. It was a local track that avoided the main highway and passed through a beautiful and varied landscape. I bounced along it on my way in and out of Pulardi then: out along the side of the community, past the old stockyards, down through a river bed, around several bends, beside huge rocky outcrops, over big bumps, through another river bed, around a final corner and up the straight and narrow stretch that delivered me back to Mount Allan.

At some point along that track was a bloated dead cow whose stench announced its impending presence long before you came across it. Oddly, I grew to know and like the reek of that rotting cow whose slow deterioration I witnessed over the course of the following year. It was part of the rich and real tapestry of desert life. I guess where I come from there's a work team to quickly remove unsightly dead cows from the sides of suburban highways. Not that there are any.

On dead cows: I remember swimming in a dam one time, not far from the community. It was a large body of water that had formed from recent heavy rainfall. Life in the desert rejoices after rain and makes use of what is provided while it can. That includes groups of people whooping it up in impermanent swimming holes. I'd had a bit of a duck dive and a splash around and was clambering up the bank on my way out when my leg brushed past something in the water. I put my hand down to feel what I was wading past and pulled up a handful of the loose flesh of a dead cow. I didn't feel anywhere near as poetic about that.

6

I bumped into Doro outside the shop one afternoon.

'Linda Nampijinba,' she called me. 'Would you like to come around for dinner tonight?'

'I'd love to.'

'It won't be much. I don't know what we're having.'

'It'll be great,' I replied. 'I'll come about six.'

Doro greeted me at the door and led me down her cool, dark hallway into the retreat.

'I bought a new painting today,' she told me, unrolling a rather large canvas. 'It's by Don Morton.'

Don was a senior man of the community, respected, affable and the father of Loretta and Blackie.

I shook my head. 'I can't believe you've bought another one,' then 'Wow,' as she spread it out to show me.

It was a large painting done on linen canvas, about two metres by one metre. It had a design that was repeated about fifteen times across the canvas. The design was a circle inside a circle inside a circle. Around the outside of each set of concentric circles was a set of horseshoe shapes.

'It's a corroboree,' Doro told me, then at my quizzical look she continued, 'The concentric circles are fires. The horseshoe shapes are people sitting around the fires.'

'These are people?' I asked, pointing to one of the horseshoe shapes.

'Yes. They're always people in these paintings. It's like looking down from above. If you look down on people from above and they're sitting cross-legged on the ground that's the shape they'll make.'

There was something dynamic about this painting. I'd seen quite a few of them by then but this one, Don Morton's corroboree, had a special quality.

'Where are you going to put it?' I asked, looking around at her walls, already brimming with smaller pieces than this one.

She shrugged in her nonchalant way. 'I'll just rearrange them all. Or maybe I'll start putting them on the roof.'

I glanced skyward. I could imagine kicking back in Doro's hobbit hole, listening to some floaty music and getting lost in this mysterious world of art.

'Drink?' Doro announced, producing a bottle of wine.

It felt a bit shocking and illicit. The consumption of alcohol was forbidden at Mount Allan.

'We'll just keep it to ourselves,' she shrugged. 'I don't think people mind if we have a quiet drink at home. We're not going to go out making trouble.'

We must have been dry. We drank the first then polished off another that night.

It was magic living at Mount Allan but it was challenging too and sometimes a tipple and a chat with a kindred soul could help you to keep things in perspective.

1989 drew to a close with me tucked away there out bush. Mount Allan, Pulardi and the surrounding desert were at the centre of my world. The community had no telephones and just one television station at a time, determined by the central receiver. I didn't live with a television but there was one I could access at the school if I ever felt the need. I don't think I ever did. There was a radio telephone in Alastair's demountable that provided our most immediate contact with the outside world. Each lunchtime he went home and made contact with the Education Department in Alice Springs. That was one of the duties of the head teacher.

The community also received the radio, one station at a time. I heard on the news one morning that the Berlin Wall had come down. I knew that was a significant world event but I felt so detached from it and much more interested in the walls at Mount Allan or the absence thereof. I had that same disconnected experience a few months later when Nelson Mandela was released from jail. Although I knew it was of major world significance, I was more concerned with who from Mount Allan was in jail and when they would be released.

*

I went back down south for Christmas, to the leafy green suburbs on the outskirts of Melbourne where I had grown up and my family still lived. They welcomed me back with open arms and were keen for tales of adventure. I think it was about that time that they gave up despairing of the decisions I made. They had relaxed into knowing that I was happy and could take care of myself, even though I made some fairly unconventional choices.

I went back to Tasmania as well, that Christmas of 1989, to say hello and farewell to my friends down there. I lived there for nine months before I went to Central Australia. It was a special time with kindred souls who came from various parts of Australia and the world to live amongst the magnificence of the Tasmanian forests, to celebrate them and attempt to protect them from the huge logging machine that was in operation. They were free-spirited, adventurous folk.

Suburban Melbourne and the forest of Tasmania both seemed light years away from Central Australia. I felt like parts of me belonged to them all. In Central Australia, people have sometimes said to me, 'Wow, Melbourne is so far from here and Tasmania is even further.' Of the three I felt like Melbourne was the odd one out, with its multitudes of people, traffic and buildings. In the forests of Tasmania and the deserts of Central Australia there is a different sense: the spirit of being in wild spaces and a certain freedom and presence of mind that comes from living more in touch with nature.

7

Almost as soon as I returned in the New Year, Maureen came tap-tapping on my demountable door. 'Nampijinba I want to take you to corroboree tomorrow night. Young man's initiation. You want to come?'

I was thrilled. It was about as good as getting a skin name. 'I'd love to come,' I told her. 'I feel honoured.'

Maureen grinned. Over tea she told me about the ceremonies. They began three days earlier, and the women had danced all night. About four weeks before that, at Christmas time, the young initiate boys were literally grabbed, taken from their families and out bush for secret men's business where they had been ever since. The ceremonies that were taking place now were the last part of the boys' initiations into young manhood.

'What do they do out there?' I asked.

Maureen shook her head with an earnest expression on her face and shrugged. She gave me a few snippets of information with pauses between each one. 'Men's business,' she said. 'Them boys gotta learn… It's law… As they go through their lives they go through more business and learn more… Only the old mans have all the knowledge.'

'And you don't know what the knowledge is?' I asked.

'No.' She shook her head again with that same earnest expression. 'We not allowed to know. If women see, they get punished… Women got our own knowledge.'

I was bursting with curiosity and had so many more questions but I knew it was inappropriate to keep asking. The more I pushed, the less I would be told. I had to sit back, watch, listen and join in. People would share information as they wanted to, in their own good time.

Late the next day, Maureen came around and told me it was time to go. It had been an oppressively hot and heavy summer's day. Storm clouds were massing to the west. They built up and dissipated, built up and dissipated, teasing us with the chance of rain then taking it away. The desire for a proper rain that would clear the air and cool things down became an obsession and a physical ache as the atmosphere grew hotter and heavier. There'd been some strong winds and thunder and lightning in the distance. Surely now, you'd think. Surely now the storm will hit us and the change we ache for will come. But it could just as easily move off in a different direction leaving us abandoned, strung-out and cranky.

I drove around to people's camps, stopping as directed until a big group of women and children had piled onto the Education Department ute. I was aware the ute had definitely not been provided for that purpose but to say no, I can't participate, the ute is only for important whitefella business, wasn't something I felt comfortable with.

'That mob in town don't know what it's like to live out here,' Alastair once told me when I asked him about the official rules on car usage. 'We have to make our own judgements about what we think is appropriate.'

Maureen sat in the front cabin with me along with a child I'd never seen before.

'This my niece, Dusty, from Yuendumu. That's Miss Kumenjayi.'

'Hello, Dusty,' I said warmly.

Dusty was as gorgeous as all the other kids with long dark curls and those signature big brown eyes.

'Allo,' Dusty replied shyly.

There were always kids I'd never seen before, kids who belonged to big, extended families and moved around the Western Desert amongst their family members. I didn't know how Dusty fitted into the family. Was she one of Maureen's brother's daughters or one of Maureen's sister's daughters or perhaps one of Maureen's cousins's daughters that Maureen would still call daughter but I would call second cousin?

According to the Aboriginal kinship system, family relationships were different to those I had grown up with. For Maureen, her sisters' children were known as her own sons and daughters. Maureen's mothers' sisters' children, who I would call cousins, Maureen considered as her brothers and sisters. So their children, who I would call second cousins, were known by Maureen as nieces and nephews. It seemed complicated to explain but the system didn't take long, once I lived with it, to fall into place and make perfect sense. Amongst extended family there was a strong sense of loyalty and responsibility. However Dusty fitted in, she was Maureen's niece, a sweet girl, who sat beside me and studied me when she thought I wasn't looking, as we bounced along the bumpy track.

'*Kakarra, kakarra,*' said Maureen all of a sudden, indicating to the right. *Kakarra* meant west. People used those words for direction as easily as I used left and right.

I pulled up abruptly because we'd almost gone past the turn. Squeals and exclamations came from our passengers in the back who had been thrown around by the sudden braking.

A little way along this track someone tapped on the back window and hollered out.

'They wanna stop for mo,' Maureen told me, gesturing with a hand sign that meant the same, the first finger flicked out along the thumb a few times.

I pulled up and several people jumped off the tray back, headed out in to the bush, returned and got back on board. Even old women moved with agility up and down off the back off the ute and out to squat in the bush. I could never imagine my mother or aunties or other senior members of my family moving in the same way.

About ten kilometres further on, we arrived on the banks of a sandy river bed. Many women and children were already there and the area was a hive of activity. Some were tending to soakages, holes dug into the sand of the river bed until water appeared and could be scooped out for drinking. Billies were boiling on small campfires. Some women were sitting in groups, sharing kangaroo meat and damper.

'Nampijinpa,' women greeted in their soft, warm way.

'Miss Kumenjayi.'

Kids were playing around and calling out with their usual 'Look me, look me,' as they demonstrated their range of antics.

I joined a big circle of women sitting in the river, as invited, and sat cross-legged like everyone else. A few of the women I knew by name and had regular dealings with. About half of them I knew to smile and say hello to. The others I had never seen before. I was passed a hunk of freshly cooked damper and a billycan, warm with tea. I dropped the damper into my skirt and slurped from the billy, the way the others did. It was like bush communion, I mused to myself, the flesh and blood of the dreamtime circa 1989. The tea was lukewarm, sweet and milky and not how I usually drank it. Still, in that weather, any liquid refreshment was welcome. I was conscious of people being aware of me. Would I eat their damper? Would I drink straight from the billycan as they did? Did I understand any of their language? I guess I was as much an object of curiosity to them as they were to me; a whitefella up close and doing it their way for a change. There were the usual chaos and highjinks, with women talking amongst themselves and across the group, laughing out loud and yelling to the kids.

I was aware of being the only white person in the gathering and the only one who understood little of the conversation or what was going on. I had to go with the flow and follow instructions. This was new for me, a free-thinking woman with a history of asking why and being part of the central organising committee. I enjoyed this relinquishing of control. I also felt privileged and humbled and knew this experience was all the more special for me because I was the only whitefella there.

The sun had dropped low into the western sky and taken its fiery intensity with it but the ground still radiated heat. Gusts of wind left us feeling gritty. Thunder growled and lightning flashed in the distance.

An older woman in the circle called out to some girls who were playing nearby. I couldn't understand what she said to them but it sounded like she was growling. She then turned to me, smiled and told me sweetly, 'These girls gotta dance for you.'

The girls, most of whom I knew from school, gathered together and moved towards us shyly. They stopped near me and formed themselves into two lines with five girls in each line.

'Miss Kumenjayi, we gonna dance for you,' Rosina announced, 'so you can learn.'

The older woman who had told the girls to dance started clapping in rhythm and a few others joined in. Amidst giggles and shyness, the girls jumped in time with the clapping, one way and then the other, with small shuffles of their feet. All the women were looking on, laughing and calling out. As the girls' feet shuffled, they held their hands together vertically in front of their chests and swayed their pointed elbows from side to side. The girls danced for a few minutes then collapsed in giggles onto the sand. Women were looking at me to gauge my reaction.

'You know it now?' someone asked me.

'Maybe,' I grinned and we all laughed.

Suddenly it was time to move. I don't know how anyone knew that. It certainly wasn't based on any time piece I could see.

The call came swift and urgent. 'Miss Kumenjayi, we go now,' and lots of women and children piled back onto the ute.

Again I followed instructions, bouncing along narrow tracks until we came upon the men of the community, waiting in a clearing in the bush.

I was told where to pull up and park. The women and children gathered about one hundred metres from the men and waited. And waited. Sometimes I wondered what we were waiting for and how long we would have to wait: central organising committee kinds of thoughts. I had to quiet them in the knowing that this time I was an honoured guest and it was somebody else's show to run. Thunder and lightning were still going off in the distance. The air was hot and heavy with impending rain. People spoke in hand signals and in their language then suddenly it was announced to me that the dancing had been postponed due to the chance of rain and we would go home and try again tomorrow.

The next evening, we went not to the river but back to the clearing in the bush where the men were waiting in the distance. I was invited to roll out my swag on a sheet of canvas allocated to a group of *Nampijinbas* and their children. The men were sitting cross-legged in circles on the ground, with five or six men around each campfire. There were about ten fires in all. It was the entire male population of Mount Allan; quiet, polite men I knew by name for a chat and a laugh. Out here they seemed different: proud and strong in the performance of these ancient, sacred rituals.

Everyone was silent, even the babies, and that was rare in those parts, where babies were totally indulged and allowed all the attention they demanded. Suddenly the music started. There was percussion first, a rhythmic beat, created by men pounding the earth in front of where they sat. Next came the singing, a deep, low chant in unison. It was primal and sacred and so it amused me that the percussion instruments included not only traditional wooden music sticks and rocks but also large two-litre plastic bottles: aspects of middle suburbia set amongst ancient earth worship.

The women and children rose en masse and moved towards the men. I stayed close to Maureen but at one stage I lost her, and another woman held my hand. About ten metres from the men, we stopped and sat in a semicircle. From that grouping, some women rose and formed dancing lines, ten lines long with about three women in each. They danced as one, pounding the earth with their feet in low jumping movements and swaying their arms from side to side. Dust from the ground and smoke from the fires mingled then was carried away on the wind.

The singing and percussion and dancing went on for about ten minutes then just as suddenly stopped. I was told it had been a rehearsal for the next evening when the young newly initiated men would be presented to their mothers and the men would make music while the women danced all night.

As we settled down into our swags, cold winds blew up across the desert. After the heat of the preceding days, this coldness took us by surprise. We slept in snatches, huddled together for warmth. At sunrise, as many as could piled into the ute and we went back home for the day.

On the third evening, the women gathered again in that same river bed. They decorated themselves; painting yellow ochre through their hair and on their arms and chests. The women went bare-breasted, many with large and heavy breasts, painted now with ceremonial lines of ochre. On their heads they wore bands into which they tucked feathers.

We moved to the bush camp and joined together in the same place, in the same semicircle as the previous evenings. As the music started, we moved forward. The women's dancing began. The seven initiate boys were brought forward. They were naked from the waist up, painted with ochre in similar ways to the women and they wore tall, elaborate headdresses of woven sticks.

I was enchanted by the ancient and earnest nature of the ceremony. These were the big boys I knew, who wore backwards baseball caps to school and struggled to sit still, always ready with a laugh and a bit of cheek. They seemed small and earnest now and totally obedient.

Each initiate was hoisted onto the shoulders of a woman and carried into the bush, accompanied by many other women. I was invited to follow. They were placed in a line beside their mothers, who chanted and sobbed and wailed, I think in an expression of grief at losing their boys to young manhood.

Back at the corroboree site, the singing and dancing continued. When we all returned, that stopped and everyone went back to our swags. Was that the all-night dancing? Everyone around me went to sleep so I followed suit.

When we were woken, it was still dark. Constellations had moved across the sky. Several hours had passed. We moved quickly to our waiting place, dragging our swags along with us. A man came over and growled in Warlpiri and then he went away.

'Lie down,' Maureen commanded, so I followed the lead of everyone around me and lay down with bedclothes pulled over my face.

'Don't look,' I was told with total urgency; enough to dispel any impulse I had to peek out.

Next came the sound of what seemed like men circling us, stamping the earth. This went on for about ten minutes. That subsided and we were allowed to sit up. A number of fires were crackling away between where we sat and where the men were, back in position, cross-legged around their fires, making music.

The women danced for the rest of the night. Not all the women danced all the time. You could sit to the side, in the audience, and join in as you wished.

'You dance, Miss Kumenjayi,' women urged.

I was reluctant. I could imitate the movements of their feet and their arms but I didn't really know what I was doing or understand what it meant. I felt a bit like an imposter. The encouragement continued so eventually I did dance.

After a while, I climbed into my swag that was out in the wings and to those ancient sounds of the chanting and the pounding I drifted off to sleep.

Next thing it was daylight and I was being roused. I was glad I had closed my eyes for a while so I could open them afresh to this amazing scene. The little campfires still flickered, the men still sat around them making music and the women continued to dance.

Suddenly the painting by Don Morton that Doro had shown me came to life. The circles were the fires. The black horseshoe shapes around them were the men sitting around the fires. The field of tiny dots was the desert landscape. For the first time, I really understood one of those paintings and could read the ancient iconography as clearly as if I was looking at a still life or landscape painting.

'Kumenjayi, you have to take the old women and children back home.'

As a rich orange glow spread across the horizon and the sun appeared as a glowing ball I drove the ute back home, laden up with women and swags then put myself to bed for the third time that night.

The next night, Thursday, was the finale. It was then that the men danced and the final acts of initiation took place. Maureen was unwell. She didn't arrive at the right time to take me so I missed out. That's generally how life was out there. Things might happen. They might not happen. I learnt to go with the flow and just be satisfied with what was. And I was satisfied. What I'd seen had been amazing. Way before the English even knew about the Great South Land, before witches were burnt at the stake, way before the Romans were exerting their power and building their mighty civilisation, before Pompeii, the Mayans, way before Christ walked upon the earth, way way back before any of that, the Warlpiri and Anmatyerre of Central Australia were building and maintaining their own civilisation and forging a sustainable way of life in the dry interior of the driest continent on earth.

I'd earned a glimpse of that piece of human history, brought forward now into the plastic-bottle present. And I'd been invited in to do that by my friends, the people of Mount Allan. It was an honour, a privilege and a great way to return to my desert home.

8

On the days that I worked at Mt Allan School, the pattern that had been established before Christmas continued. Each morning when I arrived, Alastair held the floor and talked at me for about two hours: about the students and their private lives; about traditional ways of living and his despair at how people were turning their backs on it.

It was interesting at first and, as the new kid on the block, the information Alastair was providing me with was invaluable. But after a while I grew tired of it. I couldn't get a word in edgeways and felt agitated that school wasn't starting until ten o'clock. Also, whenever a visitor came out to see us, Alastair would grab hold of them, invite them to spend time with him and chew their ears in the same way that he did mine. I would hardly get a look in. We all needed visitors out there. I was enjoying getting to know the people of the community and feeling my way at the school but the situation with Alastair was becoming hard to bear.

By April, I was floundering. I requested a few days off via radio telephone and headed into Alice Springs. The regional staffing officer was Sue Davey, a woman I liked and had a bit to do with at the time of my appointment. I went to Sue with my troubles.

'Have you talked to him?' she asked me after hearing my story.

'No,' aghast at the thought of confronting anyone in that way. I'd inherited the English way of speaking in euphemism and behind people's backs.

'Well, you have to,' she went on. 'It's the only way. Go out and tell him what you've just told me.'

The idea terrified me but I could see no other way.

On my first morning back at school, I walked into the demountable to find Alastair seated beneath the Queen. He started, perhaps with even more fervour than usual, to make up for lost time.

I pushed myself out of my comfort zone and through his chatter. 'Alastair, I need to talk to you.'

He stopped mid-sentence and asked why. I told him all I had told Sue Davey, the talking, the hogging of visitors, not starting school until ten o'clock; as honestly and professionally as I knew how. It wasn't so difficult once I got started.

Alastair listened. He asked me how I would like to do things. To his credit and my edification, things changed. Also, from having vented my concerns and being heard, I was able to deal better with the way he was. Alastair never stopped talking. He loved visitors and had a good lend of their ear whenever he got the chance. I found him to be a bit old-fashioned with more than a touch of paternalism. But he was easy-going and supportive; he had a wealth of experience and a wonderful sense of the ridiculous.

Being thrown together to live and work in such close quarters was bound to have its difficulties. All over the Western Desert, teachers who were living and working in similar circumstances were falling apart or moving on. Alastair and I muddled through.

*

Officially, the main thrust of our work was to teach English as a second language. The system we were to use was called Concentrated Language Encounters. I got the impression that the specialists who supported us in the delivery of Concentrated Language Encounters saw it as the panacea to the learning needs of children in remote areas. If we followed their instructions and delivered this program according to the script, every child would learn to read and write and we'd all live happily ever after. In reality, it didn't quite work like that and I don't think it was because we weren't trying hard enough.

We chose a big book that became our main text for a while. A big book was about a metre tall and three-quarters of a metre wide. It had large print and colourful illustrations. Having been trained in Concentrated Language Encounters at a two-day induction workshop earlier in the year, I offered to conduct the introductory session. One of the big books we had available to us was *Mrs Wishy Washy*.

The students all sat on the mat and I sat on a chair in front of them with the book propped up on a chair for all to see. First we assessed the front cover – author, title, picture, what the book might be about. Next we went through it page by page, looking at the pictures and speculating about the story.

'What's happening here?'

'Cow,' one student called out and then others joined in.

'Cow. Cow.'

'Yes, what about the cow?'

'Dirty.'

'Yes, the cow is dirty. And what happens then?'

'Wash 'im, wash 'im, she bin wash 'im.'

'Yes, the woman washes the cow.'

Laughter all round at the absurdity of it.

The protagonist was a plump, white woman who didn't like her farm animals getting dirty so one by one she washed them in a tub. 'Just look at you,' she screeched. 'Into the tub you go. Wishy washy, wishy washy.'

It had simple, repetitive lines and a nonsensical story that was completely removed from our students' lives.

We also examined linguistic features.

'What's that word?'

'She,' one of the more capable readers announced, then everyone else followed suit.

'She. She.'

I then covered up the 'e' to focus on the 'sh'. 'What sound do these two letters make?'

Silence then one of the senior students had a go. 'Sh.'

'Sh. Good. What other words have that sound?'

Kids volunteered if they could think of any.

'Shoe.'

'Excellent.'

'Sharon, Sharon,' all attention on Sharon, who looked pleased with herself for being a topic in our English class.

'Yep, Sharon. Anything else?'

After they'd thought of all the words they knew that started with the 'sh' sound, we went through the story looking for any others.

A range of activities came with Concentrated Language Encounters. Mostly they involved us making up resources: flash cards with words from the story printed on one side with which we could play various word recognition games, worksheets with fill-in-the-blank and matching activities. There was a class set of regular-sized copies of the book that students could read to each other.

Learning to read and write was a long, slow process. Many of the kids didn't attend school regularly. Even for those who did, literacy was an alien concept that they had to develop an understanding of in a language that was foreign to them. Many of them had poor hearing and other ongoing health issues. We had limited resources that we supplemented with whatever we could scrounge or invent. The school setting was so very different from the students' home environments, and their teachers were largely foreigners who passed through their lives, with very different cultural perceptions and codes of conduct from their own. For a lot of our students, their parents had either not attended school or had negative school experiences and didn't place much value on its worth.

Despite all the obstacles, many of them did turn up regularly and we did our best to make school a safe and happy place where they would want to come. Sometimes we held discos after hours. I had a cassette tape at the time of the Bangles that featured the tracks 'Walk Like an Egyptian' and 'Just another Manic Monday'.

Simple, repetitive lines that could be used interchangeably. I had to wonder about the headway we were making when I heard Loretta walking along one day, singing to herself, 'Wishy washy manic Monday.'

*

Groups of schoolkids used to visit me at home. If I was inside, they knocked and came bowling in like a flock of noisy finches. They'd be opening my cupboards, sticking their heads inside my bedroom door, using the bathroom, checking everything out.

'Your house clean, Miss Kumenjayi.'

'Your house good one.'

Sometimes it was hard for me to understand why people didn't just keep their houses clean or eat the healthy food options once we'd told them what they were. I pondered this and sometimes discussed it with others. Whitefellas spend a lot of time talking about Aboriginal people when no Aboriginal people are present. Exchanges went something like this.

'Why don't they keep their houses cleaner?'

'Because they're lazy and good for nothing.'

'Because so many people live in each house that it's too hard to keep them clean.'

'Because people are depressed and unwell from the changes that have been forced on them.'

'Because people aren't obsessed with hygiene and germs the way we are.'

'Because only a generation ago their ancestors were nomads who lived in caves or humpies or just outside in the open air. They had no surfaces to clean, no porcelain bowls or floors to wash and they didn't put down roots in one place.'

'Yeah, but now they've got houses and if you don't keep them clean you get sick. So why don't they keep them clean?'

'Because people's behaviours and ways of thinking are firmly entrenched and intergenerational. That's what culture is. You can take people out of their background but you can't take their background out of the people. Change comes slowly. It takes generations. And you can't just bash people into submission.'

On and on it went, with perspectives differing depending on who you spoke to.

'We wanna look photos,' the kids would say.

I'd get out my albums and they'd pore over them, sitting on my one big armchair, squashed in all over each other.

They delighted in looking at the album I was making of Mount Allan, taking in every minute detail, pointing things out and squealing with laughter. They enjoyed photos of my former life too: my old blue Holden once covered in snow in Tasmania that now traversed the dusty desert roads. They closely examined photos of my family and insisted on knowing who everyone was and what was going on in each shot. At photos of my mother, they exclaimed, 'Same, same,' delighting in the strong family resemblance.

'Where your mudder?' Alison asked.

They all stopped then, keen to hear the answer.

'She's in Melbourne,' I said.

'Oh, too far,' Jeremy observed, shaking his head with a look of deep concern on his face. 'She should come here, lib wid you.' Then he seemed to get another idea and added, 'Or she don't like to come here?'

'She might come for a holiday,' I replied, 'but I don't think she'll come here to live.'

'*Wiyarpa*. Poor thing,' Jeremy replied, shaking his head like he was troubled by the distance we lived apart.

Invariably the kids wanted to make scones. 'Stons,' they called them. 'We wanna make stons,' all eyeing me expectantly.

If I had the time and the inclination or couldn't resist their big, brown hopeful eyes, I agreed to an impromptu cooking session.

That led to a flurry of activity. Rapid washing of hands at the kitchen sink or in the bathroom, rummaging through my kitchen cupboards for the equipment and ingredients we needed, grubby little fingers rubbing in the butter (no matter how hard they scrubbed there were always traces of that ingrained dirt), sneaking tastes of raw dough, whoops too much milk, add some more flour, whoops too much flour, pour in a bit more milk.

Cooking involves hygiene, budgeting, measurement, nutrition, language skills, teamwork. It's a whole lot of curriculum areas rolled into one. Cooking scones at home was an out of school activity that felt at least as educationally valid as any lesson I planned and taught in school.

We slid the trays full of doughy little balls into the oven then cleaned up.

'I wanna wash, I wanna wash,' and one of the big kids would muscle their way into the sink and grab the dishwashing sponge before anyone else could.

'Dry,' someone else would cry, grabbing the tea towel.

Cleaning up in my home was a novelty. Under my supervision, a dishwashing team was appointed and everyone who missed out on that went back to poring over the photos and anything else they found interesting around my house.

One of the things they found interesting was the colour of my skin. Kids pressed on my arms and delighted in how the skin colour changed, from skin tone to paler where they were pressing. They squealed and exclaimed and call others over to check it out and have a go. If I pressed their skin, it stayed the same brown colour and didn't alter under pressure. But the cultural exchange I did delight in was pressing their little noses that gave way and squashed flat onto their faces, without the cartilage of Whitefella noses that kept them pointy and upright.

Eventually the van was filled with the warm, delicious aroma of scones and they'd be ready to come out. By then we'd be dying to get at them, split them open and pile them high with jam and cream.

The scones always tasted fantastic, soft and fresh from the oven no matter how many mistakes had gone into the mixing. We had plenty of billy tea too, out of several mugs that were shared around. It was like Devonshire tea Western Desert style and, as Alastair once jokingly pointed out, civilising the natives.

9

About every third weekend, I went to Alice Springs on the Friday afternoon after school, or earlier if there hadn't been much interest in school for the day.

Out I drove along the dusty, bumpy road. I was excited every time, for another new drive, past turn-offs to places I'd only begun to hear about, past the bores and windmills and cattleyards that seemed to exist in the middle of nowhere, rumbling over grids, past Napperby roadhouse. I didn't stop there for a traveller's break, didn't feel like telling that man what I'd learnt so far.

The drive gave me time to contemplate all I had experienced since my first drive along that road. What was I doing, swimming so far outside the flags, so far away from home? I talked too, as I went along, soliloquies for an absent audience, describing and discussing the goings on, quoting things I'd heard that I now wanted to contemplate.

Dust swirled out in thick clouds behind. I hit the black tar then in place of the dust there was a dull churn along the bitumen.

Little green signs on the side of the road informed me of my progress: SH 120, SH 90, SH 85. I deliberately looked away from some before I could read the numbers. The countdown was too slow if I read them all.

What was this SH anyway I wondered at first? I was headed for Alice Springs. I pulled over for a stretch and a piss. I enjoyed squatting in the bush. It was so calm and quiet in there and hauntingly still, existing purely for its own sake. Birds called and twittered from shrub to shrub, a lizard flashed by. I nearly walked through a web on the way back to the car and stepped back just in time to admire the thick, golden thread and its weaver, a long elegant spider.

'Sorry, lady,' I whispered, my heart pounding. Beautiful as she was, I didn't fancy tangling up with her. I walked more consciously then, carefully choosing the clearings.

SH 50. I passed a Holden cruising the other way, a carload of bush folk. They all waved out the windows then were gone.

SH 35, only 35, that's nothing compared with 400, nearly there. SH. Stuart Highway, that's it. Turn right, head south, a few more kilometres and you're there. I could taste the cold beer in advance, feel it tickling my throat, splashing away the dust. A motel room or a bed at my friends' house, a movie, shops, live music at a pub in town: the urban delights. I could spend some of the money that was piling up in my bank account. Even if I lashed out all weekend, I'd still have lots left over.

Alice Springs loomed up at last – billboards, petrol stations, rooftops – and suddenly I was out of the desert and right there amongst it: traffic lanes, industrial areas, houses, streetlights and the whole material world.

There was a share house I stayed in often, near the centre of town. Tom Moore was one of the residents, a man I knew from Friends of the Earth, Melbourne. I'd bumped into Tom in town one day not long after I was first in Alice Springs and we went back to his house with a six-pack of beer. Tom and his housemates became my friends. I was welcome to stay there whenever I liked. It was a fluid kind of household where I met my kinds of people.

There was always a party to go to on the weekend at one Alice Springs house or another. There I met more young professionals who were mostly working, one way or another, in Aboriginal Affairs. I met teachers from other remote schools who, although they were my nearest neighbours, lived hundreds of kilometres away.

Amanda McMahon and Stephanie Mackie were fellow bush teachers I made friends with at that time. They were based at Hermannsburg, also known by its Arrernte name of Ntaria, a hundred kilometres west of Alice Springs. Ntaria was a much larger school than Mount Allan, with several teachers and kids divided into classes based on their age. Because Ntaria was closer to town or because it had more teachers and infrastructure, they seemed to be much more regulated than we were at Mount Allan. By all accounts, the head teacher was much crazier than Alastair and could make life difficult and complicated for the staff of that school. When I heard stories from schoolteachers at Ntaria and other bush communities, I felt lucky to be in my isolated little sanctuary at Warriyi Warriyi. On the other hand, I did feel quite cut off. Just a relatively short trip up the bitumen for those Ntaria teachers and they could access, each weekend if they wanted to, all the support and comforts that the township of The Alice had to offer.

We developed an informal remote teachers' network and met up some weekends in Alice Springs as well as out bush, in some of the best camping spots in Central Australia. There was a passing parade of people who did their stint and then moved on. There is also a core group from that time who made Alice Springs their home, who still get together for social gatherings that have generally tamed down as the years have gone on, and whose kids have grown up together.

There's a tendency to look back through rose-coloured glasses but I do think there was a lot more optimism and room to move in Aboriginal Affairs in those days. There seemed to be greater unity and empowerment, with such political developments as the 1988 bicentennial protests in Sydney, the Aboriginal and Torres Strait Islander Commission (ATSIC), a number of recently formed key Aboriginal organisations run by and for Aboriginal people, and land rights high on the national agenda.

Education was progressing too, with bilingual programs being supported and funded and movements towards independent Aboriginal schooling taking place at various locations around the Territory. There was money for arts and innovation, for work on Indigenous languages, for music. We had Rock Against Racism, Rock Without Grog, Sing Loud Play Strong. There was Coloured Stone, the Warumpi Band, Blackbela Mujik, Yothu Yindi, and Hawke and then Keating running the country. It felt strong and exciting to be part of those things with the sense that great change was underway.

*

I met Rory in a second-hand shop. He and his mate were running it together. I was a girl from the bush, on a visit.

'Can I help you?'

'I don't know. Can you? I'm not sure what I'm looking for.'

Rory had an idea. I was fit, tanned and confident, wearing a short blue skirt and shimmering singlet top the likes of which I wouldn't have dreamt of wearing out bush. We flirted and chatted each other up until there was only one mate running the shop for the rest of the day while the other one was out with me. Then every third week when I came in I stayed with Rory, upstairs at the second-hand shop, and we did things together that seemed cosmopolitan and sophisticated compared to my life out bush; lattes, cocktails, dinner dates and dancing.

Years later, way after it was all over and I was living in Alice Springs and he had moved to Adelaide, Rory was coming to visit.

'What's he like?' my housemate asked me.

I told her he was like Mick Jagger and we laughed.

Later, when he was gone, she said she could see what I meant. He wasn't quite as sexy and his lips weren't as big but he had some of that swagger and style.

I had other boyfriends in Alice Springs too. Some of them came out to visit me at Mount Allan. None of them lasted a whole long time. Maybe it was because I was living out bush or maybe I didn't take it seriously enough. I was twenty-seven and lots of people my age were looking for partners to settle down with. I think all the really nice men I had flings with at that time did go on to do that. It would have been smart of me to do the same but I had a different path to follow.

10

It was just after three o'clock and the kids, having been dismissed for the day, had all gone running, walking or limping out of the school grounds. Some of them weren't so keen and we had to encourage them to leave.

'No, we need some time to talk now, just the adults.'

Scowling, the last ones trudged off.

After seeing them off, Maureen, Alastair and I went back inside for our afternoon debrief.

'*Nalija*? Tea?' Maureen asked, filling the electric jug.

'Love one,' Alastair replied.

'Yes, please.'

Over our cups of tea, we discussed how our lessons had gone that day.

'Why did Samuel hit Jeremy then go home so upset?' I asked Maureen. It had happened late in the day and I hadn't had a chance to find out.

'Samuel, *Wiyarpa*,' poor thing, she replied. 'Jeremy bin hit Samuel's boil.'

Samuel's boil was an angry, simmering abscess that had been building under his skin for a couple of weeks. It wasn't huge but you could see the red inflammation under his skin, spreading out from the epicentre. It looked like a big pimple but I knew from experience that it would have hurt like hell. I'd never had boils in my life until I went to Warriyi Warriyi but was now getting one every few weeks. They started out as a prick of pain under the skin and grew into painful, debilitating eruptions. If someone accidentally knocked it, you did feel an immediate and angry desire to lash out, no matter how accidental it was or how sorry the person was.

'Samuel's been getting a lot of boils lately,' I commented.

'*Yuwayi*. He should go clinic. Sister coming tomorrow.'

Once a week, a nursing sister came from Yuendumu to run a clinic in a demountable van. The sister bandaged boils and handed out a dose of antibiotics. It seemed to me that what Samuel really needed was a diet full of fresh fruit and vegetables, some vitamin pills and more hygiene in his life. The rest seemed to me like Band-Aids that were applied to so many situations out there that needed more careful and sustained solutions.

'How about Loretta?' Alastair asked. 'She was like a new girl today.'

'Wasn't she?' I smiled. 'She was all clean and bright. She did really good writing.'

Alastair nodded.

'I had a talk to her yesterday,' I continued. 'I asked her what she had for breakfast. She didn't have anything. I told her to have breakfast before she came to school because it would help her learn.'

'*Yuwayi*,' Maureen replied.

'So did she have breakfast today?' Alastair asked.

'Yes,' I told him. 'I asked her. She told me she had Weetbix.'

Maureen laughed. 'I saw her buying them in the store yesterday afternoon.'

I was pleased and amazed that my little piece of advice to Loretta had been heeded and that it had made such a difference to her. When I was a schoolgirl, my mother took care of me having breakfast. She bought the Weetbix and made sure I ate some before I went off for the day. It was barely a conscious act, just something you did that your ancestors had done before you that had proved its worth and become part of your cultural practice. I only knew enough about what went on in Loretta's life to know it was entirely different to mine.

'It's amazing what a difference little things will make,' I observed.

Alastair nodded thoughtfully. 'What's little to you can be huge to someone else,' he replied.

'What will we do in maths tomorrow?' I asked.

We'd been focusing on classification, one of the maths learning areas of the curriculum. Today we had divided the students into mixed age groups, given them magazines and told them to cut out pictures of animals, group those animals in some way then paste them onto sheets of paper, in their groups. They could draw in extra animals too. Categories that the kids had come up with in their work groups included animals they had eaten, animals from the bush, animals that 'got cheeky' (snakes, dogs and ants), animals they liked, animals you could ride and animals that could travel in cars. We all erupted into laughter about that last category.

According to the maths textbook,

> The way children classify things depends on their own experiences and the way their particular culture (including language) has helped them view their world.

The book was *Mathematics in Aboriginal Schools,* another home-grown, Northern Territory Education Department publication. It had an orange cardboard cover and was held together with staples. If Shimpo's report *The social process of Aboriginal Education in the Northern Territory*, formed a theoretical framework for my work at Mount Allan School, this book on how to teach maths provided me with a practical guide, for maths and beyond.

Maths wasn't something I'd been trained to teach but had been quite successful in at secondary school. As a consequence, I had taught junior secondary maths (albeit without much confidence) during my first years of teaching. How to teach maths to infants was new territory for me. How to teach it to infants of a different culture, who spoke a different language, seemed like an almighty challenge. But I read the manuals, observed the students going about their learning and developed a feel for how mathematical concepts were acquired by our students and how this could be supported in the classroom. To have Maureen there to introduce new concepts and words in the kids' first language seemed fundamental to their learning.

When we planned and taught together, when Maureen was fully involved and contributing her ideas and insights, it felt purposeful and fulfilling, like something I understood and was capable of doing well. Team teaching. Two-way education. I sometimes thought that if they stopped paying me I'd still go to work out there each day.

'What about where the kids live?' I suggested. 'North, south, east, west. And we can use the Warlpiri words.' It was a lesson plan from the textbook. I felt pleased with myself for finding a lesson from the textbook that focused on local content.

'From where?' Alastair asked. 'North, south, east and west from what point?'

It was an idea that could work for larger communities where there were distinct directions that people lived in, radiating out from a central point. It wouldn't work so well here where most of the people lived in the cluster of houses that were generally to the west of the school.

Maureen had been sitting quietly sketching on a piece of scrap paper while Alastair and I did most of the talking.

'What about skin names?' she said in her unassuming way.

'Skin names,' Alastair repeated. 'Good idea.'

'How will we do it?' I asked.

We waited while Maureen gathered her thoughts. 'We'll tell all the kids to sort themselves into their skin groups. I can tell them in Warlpiri. *Jangalas* and *Nangalas* can go over there. *Nampijinba* and *Jampijinpa*.' She pointed to where they could go. '*Jakamarra* and *Nakamarra*.' Pointing to a different spot. 'Like that.'

'Good. That's what they have to do. Now what about talk and record?'

The maths book suggested factoring in three main components to any maths lesson: do, talk and record. It also recommended that in the planning stage, teaching staff have a go at what they would be asking the kids to do in class.

'We can talk about who is right skin for who and who is the mother and father for each group,' Maureen suggested.

'And they can tell me about it,' I replied.

'*Yuwayi*, they can teach you.'

'Then they can go back to their seats and draw it in their books,' Alastair added. 'The eight groups and names for who is in each skin group."

'*Yuwayi,* and we can write the words on the board.' Maureen had started on a diagram like the one we would get the students to do the next day. She drew several circles and labelled each one with a skin name. Then she started to write the names of the students into the group to which they belonged.

Alastair and I joined in by thinking of more students and identifying their skin group for Maureen to write down. When we couldn't think of any more students, Maureen went and got the roll to make sure we hadn't left anyone out.

She got a new piece of paper then and drew another diagram that showed how the skin names all fitted together, who parented who, who married who. It was an elaborate and exacting piece of work.

'Do all the kids know this?' I asked Maureen.

'*Yuwayi*,' she replied.

'Even little kids understand the kinship system and how they are related to everyone else?'

'*Yuwayi*. They learn about it from when they're *witabor*. Babies.'

'They're clever, aren't they?'

'*Yuwayi*,' Maureen replied. 'They're clever, our kids.' Like she had just stated a simple fact in her modest way that made you sit up and listen.

In the introduction to *Mathematics in Aboriginal Schools* was written

> As Aboriginal society is more concerned with organising relationships between people than with organising relationships between things…it will take aboriginal children much longer to achieve competence…in their acquisition of Western mathematical ideas as these are not being reinforced by the society in which the children live.

I was beginning to realise that what was generally overlooked in that way of thinking was the amazing and exciting abilities and interests of the children. Many of them could run like the wind, flip, leap, do somersaults. They were artists, musicians, actors and dancers. They generally had outstanding ball handling and hand to eye coordination skills. They could see long distances. They had heightened powers of observation and a precise sense of direction and distance. They were brave and loving and knew how to care for others and operate communally.

It seemed to me that instead of treating the Aboriginal children of the bush like they were slow learners who would 'take much longer to achieve competence', we needed to work from a position of strength and build on their skills and interests. What the students already know and are confident in has to be at the basis of any successful education program.

*

Later, as I wandered home, I came across four of the school boys absorbed in some activity that was going on up a tree. As I approached, I realised they had a young magpie lark. Holding it by one outstretched wing, they were flinging it upward. Maybe they were trying to get it to stay in a branch. When it tumbled down each time, they would catch it and throw it up again.

I felt sad for the little bird and told them so.

'*Witabor*,' was the response to this. '*Tjurlpu witabor*. Baby bird,' which I knew already and was no adequate response to my concern.

'Yes, a little bird,' I agreed. 'What are you doing?'

'It can't fly.'

That too was obvious.

'It will die if you keep doing that. Look, it needs some water.'

It sure needed something and being thrown repeatedly into a tree by a bunch of young hunters wasn't it.

'Where did you get it?' I asked them.

'Dam.'

'Not me.'

'Him.'

'He got it.' They pointed at Pulka.

'Where's its mother? Why don't you take it back to its mother, Pulka, to its nest?'

'Too high.'

'Up a tree.'

'Ah. And did you climb up to get it down?' I asked Pulka.

'No, I threw stones. It fell down.'

Their manner had changed from excitement to embarrassment as they realised that I was not impressed.

In the schools where I came from, they would have been reprimanded, perhaps marched up to the principal's office and given a dressing down, charged with cruelty to birds. Out here, things were different.

'It will die if you do that,' I told them.

The boys looked thoughtful, although what they were thinking I had no idea. She's right, we shouldn't hurt the bird? Or, these whitefellas are weird – it's only a bird? Or, if it dies, we can cook it and eat it.

I left them to decide what to do about the bird as I wandered off contemplating the attitudes towards animals of young hunter-gatherers and what business, if any, I had to impose my own sentimentality on that.

*

One morning I woke up and couldn't open my eyes. They were jammed shut with eye glue. It was a strange, sinking feeling, like I'd suddenly lost my sight. Opening your eyes in the morning is something you take for granted until you can't do it. I lay in bed and gently worked away at it with my fingers until eventually I got one eye open enough to let the light in. I was then able to get up and bathe my eyes with lukewarm water, washing away the greenish clag as best as I could. Even after that, they felt gritty and the whites of my eyes had turned vampire red.

In the city, you'd take the day off. No one wanted to see you like that and you wouldn't want to spread it around. But everyday at Mount Allan School kids came to school with bung eye, as red as mine was now or with one eye swollen and half closed. Most of them came to school daily with their green snot, running like a string of rope from one nostril or two. They'd sniff it up but it never cleared for long before streaming down again.

'Don't sniff, blow,' we'd say and we were always sending kids off to get tissues and empty their noses. We went through boxes and boxes of tissues, which were an essential tool in our teaching kit

Sometimes when kids rubbed up against me or gave me a hug, the snot was wiped off on my clothes. It was no use being precious about it. Love and snot came in one package.

'Oh, you've got bung eye,' Alastair announced when I arrived at school, like it was a bit of a joke.

'Yep,' I replied.

'You poor thing. You're really part of Mount Allan now. Are you all right?'

'Yeah, I'm right. As long as you all don't mind looking at me.'

'We've seen worse,' he laughed.

'You got bung eye, Miss Kumenjayi,' kids commented, stating the obvious, for the next few days until it was cleared up.

'Yeah, I got bung eye,' I replied.

'*Wiyarpa*. Poor thing,' they'd say with affection.

I think my bung eye brought us all that bit closer together.

11

The Paterson family kept offering to take me hunting. Or threatening to! I sometimes bumped into them, usually out the front of the shop. We shared a special connection because I'd met them first.

'We take you hunting, Miss Kumenjayi,' Shorty or KP or one of the women would say.

'Anytime,' I'd reply, and then we'd all move on.

I'd been a vegetarian for the past ten years and I cringed at the thought of eating dead animals. Hunting didn't seem like an appropriate activity for a vegetarian. On the other hand, hunting and gathering food from the bush meant so much to the people of Warriyi Warriyi. It was integral to who and what they were. They'd once hunted and gathered because that's what you did if you wanted to eat. Now that the store provided the very largest part of people's diets, hunting and gathering had taken on a whole new meaning. Bush food, including the whole process of obtaining and preparing it, provided a deep source of enrichment, not just for bodies that were weakened by the new ways of living, but also as a part of people's overall spiritual and cultural make-up.

Being able to accept their invitation to share in this vital aspect of their lives seemed far more important than my vegetarian principles that were feeling a lot like they belonged to some other time and place.

Around midday one Saturday, the ute pulled up out the front of my house. Shorty was in the driver's seat, tooting the horn. When I appeared, he leaned out the window. 'Miss Kumenjayi, we go hunting today.'

I dropped what I was doing, grabbed my Akubra and a bottle of water and headed out.

Men were squashed into the cabin of the ute. I hoisted myself up onto the tray back where the women and children were shuffling around to make room. Amidst squashed dogs yelping and jumping off, babies crying, a crowbar up someone's bum and flies in everyone's eyes, I found a little spot and sat myself down, cross-legged.

'*Nampijinpa*,' old Shorty's wife greeted me. Her face was brown and wrinkled with a frame of thick, silver hair. She looked ancient and wise, like a weathered old part of the landscape.

I smiled at her and felt embraced. A young woman caught my eye, smiled shyly and looked away. Schoolchildren chatted and laughed and wriggled around. The young woman who I didn't know slapped the children's legs and growled at them to sit still.

We headed out of the settlement, bouncing slowly along dirt roads. It can be a rough ride in the back of those utes, where the impact of bumpy roads is felt most keenly. Tightly packed as we were, we bounced en masse; sometimes big jolts that tossed us up and saw us thud down as one. We thumped and then laughed altogether.

Whenever we reached gates across the road, children would jump down and run to open them, let the ute through, close the gate and then sprint furiously to catch up. We laughed together about that too.

Over shallow dry creek beds we churned; through the dry, prickly scrubland and alongside rocky outcrops.

The landscape increased its hold on me the longer I lived there: the orange hue of the earth, the matte, grey-green vegetation, the blue sky and the clarity. When I was out there in nature, I was in my element, living in the moment and just being. Wendy Baarda, a teacher-linguist and one of my friends at Yuendumu, once told me that when you live outside you are there with whatever is going on, the breeze, the arc of the sun across the sky, birdsong. When you spend a lot of time inside, you go inside your head.

What have we done? I wondered. We've brought along this whole new way of living that we seem to be so proud of and yet it seems so destructive when looked at from the point of view of these Indigenous people. And I've come along to teach the kids…what? And what for? The ways of thinking and reading and writing of the colonisers? To help them understand us better? Whitefellas 101? To prepare them for the jobs that didn't exist on their remote homelands? How to live well in their new sedentary circumstances: health, hygiene, tuning your telly and optimising the use of all your spare time? It seemed to me it would make far more sense if I learnt from them how to live in the moment. How to be part of an extended family. How to live off the land and be content with what you had.

Sometimes it seemed that the best thing I could do out there was bounce along in the back of an old ute, laughing with women and children, on our way out to get some bush tucker.

Closer to the dry creek beds which criss-crossed the land, leaves became shinier and broad and earth tones merged from red to brown to sandy white. Occasionally came glimpses of other delights – a flock of chirping birds, a clump of desert roses pretty-pink and uncannily delicate, a bush strewn with edible berries. Their location was noted for the return trip, or for another day.

There were changes in vegetation along the way. Always golden green and dry, at times it was low and sparse, almost grassland. Other areas were much more dense and spindly trees towered over our heads and thrashed the ute as we passed. We huddled towards the centre to avoid lashings.

'Miss Kumenjayi! Rockhole!' one child called out, pointing into the distance.

I couldn't see the rockhole but I knew it would be there, nestled in some small hollow beyond the distant mounds. The knowledge of where the rockholes were was integral to survival. The children knew the exact locations of many rockholes into the distance and pointed them out as we went.

After driving for a while, I began to wonder where we were going and how long it would take. We were driving through open plain country along a track that ran beside rocky outcrops.

The ute suddenly pulled up and with no apparent communication, women and kids started to alight.

'Come, we stop here,' Shorty's wife told me. 'Men go further.'

Blankets and crowbars, and all the other equipment we'd been nestled amongst, were tossed off to form a pile on the ground. As soon as that was done, the men drove slowly onward.

A couple of older women took off north-west, across the plain, with digging sticks and dilly bags. Something was said, something brief and rapid in Warlpiri. Some others went north-east. I was left with the young woman who'd smiled at me earlier, and the kids.

She came up and softly touched my arm. 'Here.' She handed me a billycan and a crowbar.

I smiled to myself. What on earth was I to do with them? Suddenly I felt like a fish out of water; an awkward, urban vegetarian.

'We go this way.'

We walked along, crunching over dry foliage, kids in tow and running here and there around us. As usual, the kids came alive in the bush. They raced across ground I walked tentatively over; they with their bare feet, and me in my sandals. They chattered, giggled, called out, so much more confident and at ease here than they were in the classroom.

I was the student today, out with my various teachers. We meandered along in the warmth of the late May sunshine. The air was cool and we relished the warmth from the sun now rather than trying to avoid it. Back in those intense months of summer heat, I couldn't have imagined that one day I would welcome the warmth of the desert sun.

'Miss Kumenjayi, over here,' some kids called to me. They had run off and were squatting down around something on the ground.

I wandered over to them.

'Here, here, is good, you try.' Someone handed me a little yellow fruit they'd picked from a low, ground covering plant. It was slightly bitter, with seeds in the centre, something like a cherry tomato.

'Is good?' Watching me, waiting for my reaction.

I smiled. 'Yep, it's good all right.'

That made them smile; happy that I liked their offerings. Kids kept picking and eating, as many as they could. They looked around and ran to other plants nearby that bore the same fruit. Some gathered up the fruits in their T-shirts or stored them in pockets to share with others later.

'Miss Kumenjayi, ober here.' Another group of children was gathered around a shrub, picking fruit and stuffing it into their mouths.

I sauntered over. It was a thick shrub, covered in little black berries.

Gracie, who came and went from Mount Allan and rarely came to school, glanced shyly at me and gave me a little smile. 'Here, Miss Kumenjayi,' she said softly, handing me some of the little berries. They were about the size of blueberries, slightly sweet but not terribly flavoursome. Alastair had told me they were highly nutritious and I imagined I was taking little natural vitamin tablets; shots of goodness.

'Thank you, Gracie,' I said gently, infected by her own softness.

She nodded, looking down at her feet. She was slender with slightly lighter coloured skin than most of the kids, as if she had a touch of European ancestry. She had long, stringy hair bleached blonde by the sun and big brown eyes that seemed somehow beseeching.

'What's this called?'

'*Marnakitji*,' Gracie told me.

I repeated the word after her, trying to say it in exactly the same way. I thought I was but she kept saying it and insisting I repeat it until she was happy with my pronunciation.

'Miss Kumenjayi,' she said affectionately, and put her arm around my waist, which was where her arm came up to on me.

I put my arm back around her.

'Come to school next week, Gracie,' I told her. 'I like it when you come to school.'

'All right,' she whispered.

Next we were called from another direction, more urgently. 'Miss Kumenjayi, Miss Kumenjayi, *yaraju*. Come quick.'

We all headed over in the direction I was being called.

'Nangala might get 'em goanna.' Nangala, the young woman, was crouching over a burrow which ran at an angle down into the earth.

She motioned to me so I moved slowly and quietly over and squatted down beside her.

'See, look, tracks,' she whispered, pointing at the entrance to the burrow.

I could see tracks, the little footprints of the lizard that was presumably still inside. Nangala started to dig into that burrow and soon we were staring at the rear end of a goanna. A kid squealed as Nangala reached in, grabbed the goanna by the tail, pulled it out swiftly and cracked it down onto the hard earth, once, twice then placed it, suddenly limp and lifeless, into her billycan.

The kids chattered excitedly, in Warlpiri to Nangala and broken English to me. Nangala watched me for my reaction. It was complicated. I loved being out there on the land, I loved those people and the way they were. I respected their culture, their knowledge of the land, their hunting practices. I loved the lizards too, their freedom and independence, the way they lived their own lives, minding their own businesses, fitting into the natural scheme of things. I'd just seen one being flogged to death. I definitely wasn't used to it. I wouldn't want to do it myself but I also admired the *yapa* and their ability to do that.

We stuck together as one hunting party, following Nangala. She caught two more goannas and dropped them into my billycan. We smiled. My billycan had to be put to some use.

'You right?' she asked me softly as she dropped them in.

I nodded, 'Yeah.'

'Come on, we go back,' she told me.

We wandered back with the kids trailing along, some of them bouncing around in excitement. Gracie had stayed quite close to me since our earlier exchange. I was sometimes aware of her watching me and I wondered what she was thinking.

Some of the other women were already back at the starting place, sitting beside a crackling fire, roasting the lizards they had caught. One of them was mixing up some flour and water, a dash of baking powder, a splash of salt into a big, shallow, enamel bowl. She mixed and kneaded those ingredients into a big, round damper. That was laid gently in a shallow basin amongst the coals, sprinkled with a layer of flour and covered over with ashes then hot coals. Nangala added our lizards to the collection and soon the older women returned and added their lizards to the catch. The lizards roasted in the coals. They'd changed form from vibrant creatures charged with life to limp, dead things. Now, cooked, they were little hunks of roasty, toasty meat, ready to be eaten.

We heard the Toyota returning. As we sat around our small fire, the men dug a deep hole and beside it lit a roaring blaze. They tossed their catch, a big kangaroo, into the fire, left it there briefly, and then hauled it back out and scraped off the fur with sticks. Into the deep hole they then placed the kangaroo and covered it with dirt and coals. The kangaroo's bony paws stuck out at the top, pointing skyward. Lots of little things were done that I had no idea about the first time I saw them: cooking the guts, breaking the legs, savouring the tail full of tasty fat. The tail and guts were special delicacies.

I took it all in, learning not by verbal instruction but by observation. It was the way my students had learnt to learn, not by talk and chalk, not by answering questions to which the teacher already knew the answer, but by watching. I needed to think about that in terms of my own teaching practices: less talk and more modelling.

For entree we had goanna, tea and damper, all shared out in ways that seemed quite arbitrary but I grew to understand were ritual and thoroughly controlled. After what seemed like a couple of hours, the kangaroo was removed from the earth oven, hauled up by the protruding legs. It was divided up and handed around, again in what seemed like quite a chaotic kind of a way but I knew was actually far from arbitrary. Disciplines, set in stone, had been passed on, since time began. Toyotas, rifles and crowbars had replaced more traditional hunting technologies but the essence of the rituals remained intact.

I ate, tentatively at first, with eyes upon me, breaking my private, decade long meat fast. The goanna meat was soft and white. It tore apart easily and melted in my mouth. It was a bit like a cross between chicken and fish. The kangaroo was red meat, strong and hearty.

Eating meat after all those years wasn't as bad as I thought it would be. And it seemed like the best way to start eating meat again: from animals that ran wild and free and were dropped respectfully, with a minimum of pain and anguish.

Our feast drew to a close as the sun began to set. We threw all that we wanted back into the vehicle, piled in ourselves and bounced back along the tracks, the way we had come.

Sunset out there was an artistic performance, renewed each day. This afternoon the sky was perfectly clear with not a cloud in sight. As the sun dropped lower towards the horizon, the western sky was bathed in a gentle glow and splashed with muted watercolours, pink fading to orange that grew deeper as the night sky advanced.

'Look,' I gasped as we rocked along in the ute.

My companions glanced briefly in the direction of the sunset but didn't seem impressed. I guess they saw the sunset most days so it wasn't something they got excited about the way I did.

My first hunting experience had certainly whetted my appetite for more. I felt a little more connected with the place and its people now as I did with each new experience.

Shorty did the rounds of the community, dropping people off here and there.

At my place, I jumped out and stood at the driver's door. 'Thank you, old man,' I told him sincerely. 'We go again next weekend?'

The passengers who remained all laughed at that. But I think they got the gist of what I was saying.

12

Gracie came to school the following Monday morning.

'Gracie, good to see you,' I told her.

She beamed and sidled up close to me until we were just touching. She was wearing the same clothes she had on when we went hunting, a floral skirt and a dirty crumpled, T-shirt. Her feet were bare and her hair was knotted and tousled. 'We went hunting, hey, Miss Kumenjayi?' she said in her soft way.

'Yes, and you gave me *marnikitji*.'

'Is good?' she asked me, curious.

'It's really good,' I answered her, 'and it's really good that you come to school.'

She looked up at me and gave the kind of warm, trusting, beautiful smile that made the whole thing worthwhile.

*

That morning we decided to take the students to the river bed for literacy. It was a clear, still morning. The kids always liked to get out bush and the staff enjoyed the variation in routine. Literacy in the river bed seemed to combine the best of both worlds; getting the students to think and speak in write in English but to do that in their environment, where they became the experts. In this way, education became more of a two-way cultural exchange.

At first, I never thought about all that. It felt instinctive to get out of the classroom and take the students into the bush. Later when I thought about it pedagogically and read about theoretical aspects of Indigenous education, I realised the deeper meaning of what we were doing. Events like bush trips were entirely legitimate practice that enhanced the educational experience. They also happened to be enjoyable experiences all round. It was a win-win situation.

The kids crowded into the back of the ute and we drove to a nearby river bed. As soon as the ute came to a stop, they all jumped off and ran, into the river or onto the fertile flood plains.

'Miss Kumenjayi, look me, look this, look ober dere.'

Lively and enthusiastic as they nearly always were, those kids took on new life in the bush. Some did somersaults and handstands then collapsed laughing onto the sand. Some climbed trees then jumped off boughs or sat down on the sand and play a game they called nines that involved drawing up a grid that they moved stones or berries around in calculated moves. Others dug down into the sand and produced little edible yams. Those who headed off into the bush returned with bush tucker of one sort or another. They displayed their fare proudly, holding it in the palms of their hands for me to see.

'*Yalka*,' they'd say, or '*Yiparli*,' patiently teaching me the names of the bush foods they had collected.

I had to repeat the words until they were happy with my pronunciation and then I got to eat some.

Sometimes they came back with bush medicine too and explained how it was prepared and what ailments it would cure.

'You gotta boil this up with water for sores,' someone told me, proffering branches from the prolific *warriyi warriyi* bush.

'You can boil this one and smell it, for colds.' That was the native lemongrass that grew near rocky outcrops.

Some of the keener students rifled through the pile of exercise books we had brought until they found theirs. Then they found themselves a niche, on a rock or on the sand, and attended to writing. Others needed more encouragement. Eventually everyone had found their book and a place to sit and do their writing:

'We came to the river to do our writing today and we got *yalka* for Miss Kumenjayi to eat and she said it was good and then Pulka got some *yiparli* and then he fell over and everyone laughed.' Or 'I fell over in the sand' or just a picture.

We encouraged them to write freely and the fact that they were having a go was way more important to us than getting everything right. Unfortunately the kids didn't see it that way. They were obsessed with making no mistakes.

'Is this right, is this right?' they'd ask.

They all struggled with punctuation and even the best of our writers who could put together a page of thoughts linked them all together by using 'and' rather than using full stops or commas. I felt obliged to tell them the truth, even though it interfered with their flow. If any part of it was wrong, they would insist on an eraser to rub out any mistakes and fix them up.

'Just cross it out,' I'd say, 'put a line through it and write the new word next to it.'

But they wouldn't hear of it.

Some of the older male students had been through initiation and in their culture were seen as young men. In their eyes, school was for kids, which they were no longer, but the laws of the nation required that they continue to attend. Also, they were too young for work or CDEP so there was nothing much for them to do if they didn't attend school. Schools on larger communities were able to run targeted programs for older students. It was difficult to do that at Mount Allan with our limited size and resources. The best we could do was treat them with respect and try to make school as meaningful as possible

One small gesture was to not refer to any of the male students as boys. To say things like 'All the boys come over here' was inappropriate if we were including older males who were no longer considered to be boys. It was better to use a more generic term like fellas or blokes.

A group of kids had finished their writing and wanted to play I spy.

'Yes, Carol, you go first.'

Carol looked pleased and shy. 'I spy with my little eye something beginning with S.'

'Sky,' someone piped up.

'No,' replied Carol.

'Sandal, sandal,' bursting with the excitement of it.

'No,' replied Carol calmly.

They all looked around for more clues.

'I know. Sand, sand,' Loretta suggested.

Carol nodded coyly. Blackie looked disappointed. She wanted to get it.

'You have my turn,' Loretta said to Blackie.

Blackie looked pleased and then shy. 'E,' she said. 'I spy something beginny E.'

'Ears,' yelled Loretta.

Blackie shook her head.

'Eyes,' said Gracie.

Again Blackie shook her head. 'E, e,' she said, trying to emphasise something about the letter.

'Elephant, elephant,' Samuel called out.

Again Blackie shook her head.

'There's no elephant here,' I said.

'Edgar,' someone said and all heads turned to Edgar, who was digging in the river bed sand, over in the distance.

'No,' replied Blackie, shaking her head.

We were stumped. 'What is it, Blackie?' I said. 'Tell us.'

She took a big breath. ''Elicopter,' she blurted out.

We couldn't see it but we could hear one whirring in the distance.

'You can't see 'elicopter,' one of the other kids insisted, like they'd been duped, looking at me for adjudication.

I didn't have the heart to tackle the bigger, phonics issue. Luckily Alastair and Maureen had decided it was time to go back.

'Everyone into the ute,' Alastair called and they all took off running to get a good spot.

*

'I might go to Yuendumu this afternoon to use the phone,' I announced on our way back to school. I was planning to enrol in a course of postgraduate study that I could do by distance education and needed to make an enquiry. It was a one hundred and twenty kilometre round trip to make a phone call but it was also a good excuse for an outing.

'I'll come too,' Maureen said in her simple, understated way.

We set off in my work vehicle, the big Toyota ute. Driving out, I was reminded what a tiny settlement Mount Allan was, in the midst of a vast desert. I marvelled at that and how I was quite content to exist within its boundaries. All the same, it was exciting to drive out of the clutches of the community and set off on an adventure, bouncing up the dusty track on our way to somewhere else.

'We go bush way?' asked Maureen.

'*Yuwayi*, you show me the way.'

'We went that way last time, remember? Go same way.'

'Yeah, but I don't remember which way it was.'

Maureen knew every stretch of road, every piece of bush, every detour, and every bush track. She knew the exact locations of bores and waterholes. So did Pulka, who was coming along too. He was about ten years of age, a regular Mount Allan student. I know teachers aren't meant to have favourites but I did have a special soft spot for Pulka. He was only distantly related to Maureen but she said his people had agreed for him to come.

Maureen laughed at me. '*Kumenjayi, wiyarpa*,' she said affectionately. *Wiyarpa* translated roughly as 'poor dear thing'.

It was because I was a suburban girl and an outsider in the ways of the bush. She'd shown me the way to Yuendumu before, the myriad of bush tracks and cunning turns but still I didn't know it. Still I needed her assistance to guide me there.

'Miss Kumenjayi, *walypala*, whitefella,' was Pulka's observation: honest and affectionate.

We all laughed.

'Here, turn here.'

I took the right turn, off the main track and down a narrower, much bumpier bush road.

'*Nyungka*,' cried Pulka, '*marlu*. Look, kangaroo.' As he spoke, he held up an imaginary rifle.

Three kangaroos that were congregating on the road ahead separated and bounded off, disappearing into the bushes. Pulka pretended to shoot them. We all looked intently but those kangaroos were nowhere to be seen. They had disappeared into the scrubland adjacent to the road.

'You missed them,' I commented, secretly pleased.

'No rifle,' murmured Pulka, disappointed.

We turned this way and that, veered with the track and passed dams, rocky outcrops and old bores. We laughed and sang and teased each other and finally, about an hour later, we turned left onto the main road into Yuendumu.

A humpy came into view, then another. They were simple lean-tos, of corrugated iron. Once upon a time, humpies had been made from branches and sticks and leaves, strategically interwoven to create little round shelters. With colonisation had come new materials which the bush people now used instead, applying the same age-old knowledge and techniques. It was the same way they had used plastic bottles at the corroboree to beat out ancient rhythms. I marvelled at the bush people's ability to innovate and adapt, which I came to realise was how they had survived for so long in this place.

There were clearings in the bush now, to make way for people and campfires and dogs. We were on the outskirts of Yuendumu, population approximately a thousand: four times as big and at least four times as crazy as Mount Allan. 'Rubbish place,' was how the Mount Allan people commonly spoke of Yuendumu. It did seem like a rubbish place with litter everywhere and broken-down buildings and social problems on a much larger scale than at Mount Allan.

I proposed that we head first for the school.

'School might be closed,' Maureen replied.

'No, it's only four o'clock. Teachers will still be there.'

As usual, Maureen's offhand comment turned out to be right.

'The school is closed, Maureen. How do you know these things?'

She shrugged and offered no explanation.

'Might be sorry,' offered Pulka. By that he meant sorry business because someone had died.

'*Yuwayi*, sorry business, one old man was sick,' Maureen told us. 'One Jangala, our father. Drop me over west camp, Kumenjayi.' She directed me to west camp, where she and Pulka jumped out of the Toyota. 'Pick us up later,' she instructed and they turned their backs.

I was left feeling mystified. I assumed that Maureen had known about this sorry business all along and that's why she wanted to go there. Instead of telling me that, she had allowed me to drive to Yuendumu to make a phone call knowing full well school would be closed and I wouldn't be able to. At times, I felt like we were developing a close and trusting relationship. Then something like this happened that made me think we were little more than strangers.

I went in search of the friends I was making there who were mostly staff from the school.

Wendy B was at home. She was a senior teacher, originally from country Victoria who had lived at Yuendumu for many years. 'Oh yes,' she said, 'old Jangala just passed away. School might be closed for days. You can use my phone.'

I appreciated her warmth and generosity, as if nothing was too much trouble. 'It's too late now. Thanks anyway. Their office closes at 4.21 on the dot. I learnt that last time when I raced up here to Yuendumu and rang at 4.25 to get their recorded message.'

'Oh dear,' Wendy replied and laughed. 'They don't know what it's like living out here, do they? Those things can be hard when you live out bush. Here, let me make you a cup of tea.'

Wendy's kitchen and whole house seemed to be a chaotic accumulation of years of suburban living in the desert. She lived with her husband and her children, now young adults who came and went with partners and offspring and complicated stories of their own, as well as a *yapa* family of parents and children and the extended family they brought with them.

A small group of kids entered the kitchen as we waited for the kettle to boil. They addressed Wendy in Warlpiri. '*Arpiliyi, kalipa yarninjaku.* Grandma, we're hungry.''

She replied in Warlpiri and they nodded enthusiastically. She then produced a loaf of sliced white bread and a caterer's size packet of cheese slices from the fridge. She buttered bread, slapped slices of cheese onto it, another piece of bread on top and handed a sandwich to each child, who then disappeared out the door. The whole operation seemed smooth and effortless, a well rehearsed routine.

Wendy was neat and trim. She was dressed in her trademark A-line skirt that fell to just above her knee, a plain T-shirt and some coloured beads. She had short brown hair that sat neat and unflustered, and wore sensible lady's sandals. Wendy appeared calm and healthy and like she cruised through life, seemingly unruffled, by the disarray that bubbled all around her.

'Do you want a sandwich?' she asked laughing.

I hesitated. It wasn't my usual fare. 'Yes, why not?'

We drank tea and ate cheese sandwiches, seated at the laminex kitchen table.

Wendy laughed the way she did, like she generally saw the humour in things. 'I bought some new cups. My mother's coming for her annual visit. She doesn't really approve of how I live here. I thought these new mugs might make her feel better about it.'

They were porcelain coffee mugs with a painting of a different Australian bush flower on each one. I looked around at the torn curtains, the built in grime, the old well-worn furniture and the general messiness of the place and felt that this set of new mugs was hardly going to make the difference. I didn't tell her that, though. I asked her about her job.

'I'm the teacher-linguist. I work alongside a *yapa* teacher, Napaljari Ross. She is a teacher-linguist too. We go around to each class and give lessons in reading and writing in Warlpiri.'

'That sounds like a good idea,' I replied, thinking about how much I would like to be doing that at Mount Allan.

'Yes, it is,' she replied. 'The kids learn to read and write in Warlpiri first, when they're little and they don't know much English. At first, most of their literacy learning is in Warlpiri. Each year the amount of Warlpiri they learn at school goes down and the amount of English they learn goes up. By the time they get to grade six, they should be competent in both.'

'And are they? Does it work?'

'Yeah.' In her trademark, hesitant way. 'It does work. They learn to read and write in their own language first then as they got older and they learn more English they can transfer their skills to English. They have to come to school, that's all. That's how school is. If they don't come to school regularly, it makes it much harder for them. But the ones who do come, they learn in both languages. It's good for the *yapa* teachers too. It makes them an integral part of the school.'

I liked listening to Wendy talk. She had a way of enunciating her words clearly and speaking in a way that was simple and humble but at the same time eminently sensible.'

'Those *yapa* teachers, are they qualified?' I asked.

I loved the idea of having qualified Aboriginal people teaching their own kids. That seemed ideal and like the way it should be. Some afternoons I stayed back with Maureen after school and worked through a guide to education for assistant teachers. I hoped that she would also do the teacher training one day. I was developing the idea that whitefellas who were working out bush should all be training local people up to do our jobs and thus be working towards our own redundancy.

'Yuendumu has eight qualified *yapa* teachers,' Wendy replied. 'Local people. They do their studies in the RATE Program at Batchelor College.'

'The RATE Program?'

'Oh yes. Remote Area Teacher Education. There's lots of acronyms aren't there? Sorry.' She laughed. 'People throw those acronyms around expecting everyone to understand them. With RATE, the graduates come out with a qualification that allows them to teach on their own community. We have a mentor teacher here too, so when the *yapa* teachers are qualified and they start teaching their own class there's someone there who can support them.'

'That's great. I wish I had a mentor teacher.'

'Yeah,' she laughed. 'I think we all do.'

A gorgeous little curly-haired girl with big, doe-like eyes came into the kitchen and sidled up to Wendy. A couple more kids stood in the doorway. The little girl whispered in Wendy's ear.

'Oh, you want cheese sandwiches too?' Wendy laughed.

The little girl nodded shyly.

'Theo, this is my friend Linda. Linda, this is Theo.'

'Hello, Theo,' I said.

Theo clung to Wendy.

'Say hello,' Wendy told her.

'Allo,' Theo murmured.

Three cheese sandwiches, one apiece, and those kids were on their way. I wondered how many kids Wendy fed cheese sandwiches to.

'Yuendumu seems really different to Mount Allan,' I observed. 'It's only sixty kilometres up the road and the people from the two communities are so related. How can they be so different from each other?'

Wendy nodded. 'Yeah, it is different. Yuendumu's a lot bigger. And there's a different history here.' She thought about it then kept going in her simple, sensible way. 'Yuendumu started off as a government-run mission. People were rounded up and brought here. Even if they didn't want to come. They had to line up for rations. There are people here today who won't stand in a queue today for anything because it reminds them of when they had to line up for food. Mount Allan was a cattle station at first. Some of the *yapa* didn't want to live at the mission. They moved in to Mount Allan and got work there. Their job might have been to maintain a bore. They could live near the bore with their family and still live off the land and do plenty of hunting. But they got rations too, and the protection of living on the station land. So the people of Mount Allan tend to be more bush people and also have more of a work ethic.'

'But we don't have any qualified teachers or other of the politically minded kinds of *yapa* that Yuendumu seems to have.'

'No, Yuendumu people have probably had more experience dealing with whitefellas,' she said in her reflective way. 'The Mount Allan people are a bit more bushy.'

A man appeared in the kitchen doorway, tall and dark with a big smile.

'Oh, Jampijinba. This is Linda, from Warriyi-Warriyi.'

'Allo,' he said and stepped forward to shake my hand. '*Kultitja mayi?* You're the schoolteacher? With Maureen?'

I nodded.

'*Yuwayi,* she's my sister,' he told me.

'This is Hudson,' Wendy said. 'He lives here, and Ursula his wife and their sons.'

'Pleased to meet you,' I told Hudson.

'Pleased to meet you too,' he replied. 'You're *nambijinba mayi?* Are you *nambijinba?*'

'*Yuwayi,*' I replied.

Hudson smiled and nodded. 'You're my sister too. *Ngurrdju.* That's good.' He shared Maureen's gentle, understated way. 'Oh well, I might go and play guitar.'

Hudson turned out to be an accomplished guitar player. Wendy and I joined him in the lounge room where he played masterfully and sang songs that we joined in on. Wendy got another guitar and they jammed together. Some of the songs were Wendy's own compositions, written in that same style in which she spoke, simple and to the point but concealing, not far below the surface, deeper insights.

I stayed until after dark and left Wendy's house feeling uplifted by the unconventional family environment and the insights into local life it offered.

*

Maureen sang out to me as I drove back through west camp where I had left her several hours earlier. 'Pulka's stopping here,' she announced, and then she read the concern in my face and added, 'Just till the weekend.

He'll be right here. You had a good visit?' she asked me as we drove out of the community and onto the main road.

We were going home via the highway. It seemed safer than the back roads at night.

'*Yuwayi*, I went visiting at Wendy B's house.'

'You met my brother Hudson?'

'Yeah. He was playing guitar.'

'He's good guitar player,' she replied. She told me about the old man who had passed away, the sorry business and various family members. We were well along the road by then.

'*Nampijinpa*, I might stop for a piss,' I announced casually.

Her reply came as a soft, low growl. '*Lawa*, you can't.'

'Why not?' Even as I asked I knew why not and nodded, mentally answering my own question. I turned to look at Maureen.

In place of her face was a pitch-black face, framed with long, sharp black spikes. It was ugly and terrifying. '*Kadaicha*,' that face hissed at me in a long and low sound, which sent an icy shiver through my body.

As quickly as it had appeared, that horrible face was gone. Maureen sat, composed. What had just happened? What had I just seen? I was too afraid to speak or to look at Maureen again. I drove in silence, haunted by strange lights and figures on the side of the road, of chill fingers creeping around my neck. Finally we turned off the main road and on to the home stretch that would take us home to bed. I was busting by then.

I dared to break the silence. 'Maureen, can I stop for a piss?'

'Yes, you can stop for mo.' Quite simply, like it was a strange sort of a question and why shouldn't I if I needed to? Like nothing at all had happened back there to frighten the living daylights out of me.

We resumed speaking then about anything except what had happened back there, which mystifies me to this day.

13

I met Baby Blue outside the store with his son Andrew. He was going gaga over someone else's baby. One of the endearing features of the men of Warriyi-Warriyi was the way they presented as strong, warrior types; reserved and a bit foreboding; but in the proximity of babies they became uninhibitedly soft and clucky.

I was with Maureen. She stopped to talk to a strong, handsome man. They conversed in Warlpiri while I stood by her side, looking down and trying to understand what they were saying. After a while, they switched to English and Maureen introduced us. He was Alan Norman, father of Andrew, but they called him Baby Blue.

'Pleased to meet you, Miss Kumenjayi. My son here, Andrew, he's happy with you.'

'Well, I'm happy with Andrew,' I replied and Andrew and I beamed at one other.

'You right here at Mount Allan?' Baby Blue asked.

'Yeah, I'm good,' I replied.

Baby Blue and Maureen had another short conversation in Warlpiri then Maureen told me, 'They wanna come over for *nalija*. Cup of tea.'

I did a quick mental calculation. I'd planned on studying that afternoon. I had finally enrolled in the postgraduate Aboriginal studies course. I'd been thinking about it since I first arrived at Mount Allan, when I thought I would have unlimited spare time on my hands. Ever since the first batch of study materials had arrived, along with some excellent textbooks that I had only managed to read snippets of, community interactions kept cropping up that kept me from my studies. Rather than learning about the Indigenous Australians from books, I was hanging out with them. I couldn't possibly and nor did I want to tell Maureen and Baby Blue, no, I don't want you to come over now. I want to go home and read about you.

Instead I told them, 'Yes, come over,' and the four of us wandered back to my place.

They arranged themselves in the fireplace area, where I sparked up the fire and put the billy on.

Baby Blue and Andrew became two of my regular visitors. Sometimes Andrew brought other kids along too. I'd be sitting in my outdoor living area, enjoying the ambience that comes with outdoor living, the breeze, the birds, the passing of time. Because the people of Warriyi-Warriyi tended to live a large part of their lives outside, there were protocols around that, just as for serial house-dwellers there are protocols around approaching someone's front door and entering their house.

'Miss Kumenjayi,' they hollered as they approached.

'Hello,' I called back.

'Is all right we come to visit?'

'*Yuwayi.* Come in.'

They arranged themselves, sometimes dragging over one of the old kitchen chairs that kicked about the place. I usually sat on my swag that was just about permanently set up outside by then.

Baby Blue was a solid man with a big personality who'd spent time in jail for aggravated offences. He had a soft, shy wife who didn't seem to mind her husband befriending me, or perhaps didn't get any choice

In my life until now, I'd never met men who were prone to any kind of violence, let alone domestic violence. They just weren't the kinds of people I chose to spend time with. But here at Mount Allan I did consort with people who had committed heinous crimes. Not only did I consort with them, I befriended them and enjoyed their company. I took them for who they were to me and didn't think about or talk about what they had done or what they did in their lives away from me. It was part of how living at Mount Allan challenged me and with things I used to think were black and white presenting themselves in various shades of grey.

Baby Blue gave me Warlpiri lessons. He was a perceptive and patient teacher and my language learning was coming along, aided by his efforts.

One day, Andrew and Baby Blue arrived just as I had finished arranging wood to make a fire.

'M*atches-ji kanpala mandarni palka*? Do you have any matches?' I asked in the best Warlpiri I could muster, enunciating slowly and carefully.

'*Nyiya? Pina wankaya*. What? Say it again,' Baby Blue replied.

My best efforts in Warlpiri and he couldn't understand me. How disappointing!

'*Matches-ji kanpala mandarni palk*a?' I asked again, perhaps even more carefully.

'*Nyiya?*' Looking at Andrew, looking at me, keen to make sense of what I was saying but getting neither head nor tail of it.

'Say it fast,' Andrew suddenly announced. 'Miss Kumenjayi, you talking too slow. Say it fast.'

I let go of my careful enunciation and repeated the phrase again, this time jabbering the language off the way it sounded to me when I heard other people conversing. This time, Baby Blue smiled and produced a box of matches from his pocket. The speed of delivery had made all the difference.

I loved these visits and the easy friendships I had with the people of this community. Here, three thousand kilometres from where I came from, amongst people of a vastly different colour, culture and linguistic background, I felt like I belonged and was accepted for simply who I was.

*

There was always something a little bit different about Thursdays, a special feeling right from when you woke up. Thursday, mail plane day, I'd think to myself. There was something in it for everyone: money which led to food and new clothes and petrol to travel around, maybe a community member who'd been away and got a lift back home on the plane. For me there was usually a box that was my weekly order of perishable food, sent out from Woolworths. Fresh fruit and vegetables, cheeses, yoghurt. The other thing I received was personal letters.

'Miss Kumenjayi, Miss Kumenjayi, mail plane day.' Rosie and Jenna had come running up to me as I was setting off for school.

'Is it?'

'*Yuwayi. Junga. Wulkamanu* day. Yes. True. It's old woman day.'

Rosie said that so seriously I couldn't help but smile.

Wulkamanu day was every fortnight. It was the day the community mail bag came with the old women's pension cheques. It contained other people's pension cheques too but it was the old women's cheques that mattered to the kids that they cared for.

'I might get new clothes.'

We headed off for school together.

'Morning, Miss Kumenjayi,' greeted old Sandy Allan on his way up the hill. 'Mail plane day.'

'*Yuwayi*, mail plane day.'

'You might get letter from your boyfriend.' My non-existent boyfriend was a bit of a joke with Sandy.

'He won't find me out here,' I told him.

'He might come here and steal you back.'

'Well, I'm not going.'

'Everything's all right?'

'*Yuwayi*, I'm happy here.'

'*Ngurrdju.*' Good. 'We happy with you, Kultitja.'

Maisy arrived to stand beside Sandy. 'Miss Kumenjayi,' she said in greeting. '*Ngurrdju?* Are you good?'

'*Yuwayi, Ngurrdju.*'

She smiled and reached out her hand to stroke down my breast. I took that as a sign of her affection.

''Ow much your car?' Sandy enquired as usual.

'A million dollars.'

More laughter.

'*Nyuru.* Okay. Have a good day.'

Further along the route to school, 'Miss Kumenjayi,' Maureen hollered out from her camp.

'Morning, Nampijinpa,' I hollered back, squinting in the brightness of the morning light to make her out.

She waved so I could see her. 'It's mail plane day, *mayi?*' *Mayi* is like 'ay?' – the end part of a question.

'*Yuwayi*, mail plane day. You coming?'

'*Yuwayi*,' and I knew she'd be along to school with whatever kids she'd collected for that day.

'Okay, see you there.'

'*Kumenjayi.*'

'Miss Kumenjayi.'

More kids ran up to hold my hands. Swinging arms together, we walked the final stretch to school.

'Miss Kumenjayi.'

'*Kinyariya.*'

'It's Tursday today?'

'Yes.'

'Mail plane come today?'

'That's right.'

'It's *walkumanu* day. I might get new clothes.'

'From your grandmother?'

'*Yuwayi*, she bin tell me.'

Finally the whirr of the small motor confirmed our hopes. The children waved madly from the school as the plane swooped down from overhead. Whatever they were doing, they stopped and ran to the windows or doors to pay their weekly homage.

People sitting down in the community, making damper or painting or woodcarving or looking after children or tending the garden or whatever else, halted momentarily to acknowledge the plane. Dogs barked. Office workers made decisions about who was driving out to meet the plane. Bags had to go too, full of outgoing mail. Occasionally people arrived or went in by plane.

At lunchtime, Alastair picked up the school mail from Janice at the office. He usually came back with some fresh outrage about something she had said or done this time. If any kids came back on Thursday afternoons, Maureen and I supervised them in the second demountable or outside in the yard, giving Alastair time to open the official mail and attend to school administration. The kids who turned up got free choice on Thursday afternoon. It might be painting or Lego construction, outside games or an educational video.

There was one film called *Flash Attack*. It was made in Alice Springs by the Aboriginal media group CAAMA Productions. *Flash Attack* told the story of a man from the bush who went into Alice Springs to buy himself a second-hand car. He bought a hotted-up, flash-looking unit that turned out to be a bomb, and slowly but surely the car fell apart. There were scenes where the door fell off in his hands and another where he kicked a tyre in frustration and it suddenly went flat. The kids squealed with laughter at these scenes, over and over again. It was about what to do and what not to do when buying a used car; consumer education presented in a local and entertaining way.

Mostly the students didn't come back because they stayed with their families for money or clothes or food or toys or all of those things. Or their families put petrol in thirsty cars and headed out, for hunting or homelands or town. Sometimes Maureen didn't come back either.

I'd be dying for school to finish so I could go home with my letters. I received about eight personal letters per week at first and always replied to them before the next Thursday, the next mail out.

At home time, I took off with my little bundle of prized possessions. No detours on mail day, I went straight home for my weekly ritual. I made myself a drink, generally of lime cordial with sparkling mineral water that I brought ample supplies of from Alice Springs, then sat down on my own, inside or outside, to pore over my letters. I laughed and cried and read my letters over and over again, missing my family and friends and gazing into the far distance, often until the sun dropped low into the western sky and I was straining to see the words.

My parents were my best correspondents and wrote weekly, as requested. Writing to them was good value because for each letter I sent to their address I received two in reply, one from Mum and one from Dad. Mum complained once that she didn't have enough news to write a letter each week. I didn't care what she wrote. I just liked her handwriting and the personality it reflected. 'Just tell me what you had for dinner,' I told her.

I had a one-letter policy. That meant I would write one letter to anyone. If they didn't reply, I didn't write again. Letters were too precious to be wasting effort on those who wouldn't reply.

14

In the relentless heat, I had strange cravings to eat very spicy food. One of my staples was a jar of hot lime pickle, normally eaten with Indian curries. I used to spread it thickly on rice cakes and find an odd pleasure in the pain of the heat.

I spent the next couple of days wearing a trail only between the bedroom and the toilet. At one stage, after yet another vomiting attack, I glanced at myself in the mirror on the way back to collapse on the bed, and my face had turned green. I'd read about people turning green but had only thought it was an expression until then, not something that actually happened.

Some kids came to visit. 'Miss Kumenjayi, you really sick,' they said. They ran and got the visiting nurse from Yuendumu.

By then I couldn't retain water.

'If you're still like this tomorrow,' she told me, 'we'll call the Royal Flying Doctor plane and have you airlifted to hospital in Alice Springs.'

By morning, I was the tiniest bit better. I could drink sips of water without them going straight through me. I stayed put and slowly improved until I was back on my feet. Eventually I resumed eating hot lime pickle again although I stopped spreading it quite so thickly.

I did love living at Mount Allan. It was rich, joyous and life-changing. At the same time, on a day to day basis, it was harsh. A former bush teacher once told me that when you lived out bush you were always either sick of being tired or tired of being sick. I related to that entirely while at the same time knowing I was having the most wonderful experience.

*

I grew particularly close to the people of Pulardi, known locally as the Pulardi mob. They often came to Warriyi-Warriyi, for mail and weekly payments that came on the plane, for shopping and sometimes just to visit. When you lived at the tiny settlement of Pulardi, then Mount Allan seemed like a township with ample resources. When you lived at Mount Allan, then the much larger community of Yuendumu seemed like a township. At that time, Yuendumu was the fifth-largest town in the Northern Territory. When you lived at Yuendumu and felt like stepping up, you went to Alice Springs.

When my closest friends from Pulardi came to Mount Allan, they often visited me and sometimes stayed the night.

Johnny Briscoe became a regular visitor. He was one of Teddy Briscoe's sons, and lived between Pulardi and Mount Allan. He was a few years younger than me, a proud, strong man who did station work as his father had done; breaking in horses and mustering cattle. JB, as he was generally known, was a great one for sitting by the fire telling stories. He often came around in the late afternoon, for a cup of tea and a yarn. Surprised by my admission that I didn't know how to ride a horse, JB offered to take me riding. Up for almost anything, I enthusiastically agreed.

The next afternoon, I met JB out at one of the distant fenced yards where some horses were agisted. JB set me up on a tall white horse that he told me was particularly 'quiet'. He rode beside me and we set off at a walk.

After a while, JB tired of my tentative riding style so he came up behind me and whacked my 'quiet' horse hard on the flank. It took off then at a cracking pace with me bouncing around loosely in the saddle and JB laughing in the background. That was the last of my riding lessons.

JB introduced me to his cousin Joe Daniels, then they often came visiting together. One day during a lull in conversation, they asked me for a story.

'Tell us story, Miss Kumenjayi. Anything.'

Nothing came immediately to mind but then I decided to tell the story of the original occupation of Australia. 'Just over two hundred years ago, Aboriginal people were living around the Sydney area the old way. Living off the land, no motorcars, no shop food, no clothes. You know, just living off the land, the old way?'

They got the picture and nodded their understanding.

'Ships sailed in from England. Those people who lived on the coast there had never seen ships before. Whitefellas were on those ships. The ships came to shore and the whitefellas got off. They didn't care about the Aboriginal people or the way they were living.'

'No, not that story,' they both said emphatically. 'Tell us a different story.'

It was hard to always come up with a story on the spot. 'Well, I grew up in a suburb about thirty kilometres from Melbourne,' I told them, 'called Mooroolbark. There were streets and houses everywhere. I lived in a house with my mum, dad, brother and sister and we had a dog and a cat and a swimming pool in the backyard. There were houses behind us and next to us, in every direction. We got to know some of our neighbours and they became our friends. We used to wear uniforms to school. I would walk for one hour to get to my high school, carrying a school bag with my lunch and my books.'

They listened keenly to my story that I thought was the most boring and ordinary on earth and shook their heads like they'd never heard anything quite so remarkable.

'Where your parents now?'

'Where your brother and sister now?'

'Who lives in that house now?'

'Are you going back to live there?'

Another time they brought up a story they'd seen on television about a kangaroo cull at a national park in Victoria. 'What are they doing with all those kangaroos?' they asked. They were practically drooling at the mouth, contemplating all that freshly killed meat.

'I don't know,' I shrugged. 'Maybe they're going to bury them all.'

The two of them looked entirely alarmed.

'What a waste,' JB said, shaking his head thoughtfully the way he did.

'We should get a van and go down to get all that meat and bring it back up here for everyone to eat.'

Brenda and the kids used to come over when they were staying at Mount Allan. Sometimes they brought their swags and we all bedded down around the fire. Or I slept beside the fire and they all lined up on my bed inside. For me, it was novel to sleep outside. For them, it was the other way around.

*

The heat of summer faded into a beautiful desert autumn. There were no deciduous trees and the seasonal pattern in the desert didn't really correspond to temperate versions of summer, autumn, winter and spring. There was, however, a period between the intense heat of summer and the chill of winter that was magnificent. The rocks glowed deep orange, radiating the heat they had absorbed through the long summer months.

Intense heat gave way to comfortable warmth. We moved through April and May into a cold time when the temperature at night dropped to below zero. Sometimes, those days would heat right up into the high twenties. At other times through the winter, the sun was weak and watery and the cold, dry air chilled you to the bone. That weather allowed for indulgence in the homely pleasures I associated with life down south: warm baths, pots of soup, snuggling under a doona.

People moved around, wrapped in blankets or whatever warm clothes were available. They didn't tend to keep clothes from one season to the next nor buy the latest winter range in advance, so a sudden onset of cold weather could catch people unawares. On winter mornings, people tended to stay snuggled in their beds until the sun was high and the air had warmed up, at least to above zero degrees Celsius. School started later as the cold weather set in, with many kids not joining us until recess time. The store ordered in a bundle of warm jackets, quilted and brightly coloured. These became the winter uniform of Mount Allan.

'What colour are you going to buy?' Doro asked me one morning when I bumped into her outside the store. She was sporting one in smart olive green: her latest acquisition.

I had a jacket I'd brought from down south and I didn't really need another but Doro was insistent. I chose smoky blue.

*

Eventually instead of driving in and out of Pulardi three times a week, the Pulardi mob invited me to take my swag and camp there.

I camped with Brenda and Michael and the kids, all lined up in swags on the ground out the front of their house. Sometimes, little Stephanie climbed into bed with me for a cuddle. We sang 'Twinkle Twinkle Little Star', her in her three-year-old voice, making up the words as she went along. She did the hand signs too, the twinkling fingers and the diamond in the sky. Sometimes she fell asleep and stayed snuggled up for the night.

At sunrise, perhaps around six in the morning, the kids woke me. 'Miss Kumenjayi, Miss Kumenjayi, time for school.'

Someone would get up and rekindle the campfire. We sat up in our swags then, all sleepy and crumpled, to eat damper and kangaroo for breakfast, washed down with tea that we drank straight from a shared billycan. After breakfast, I smoothed down the clothes I had slept in, ran my fingers through my hair and headed over to the schoolroom.

I had neither a hairbrush nor a timepiece and welcomed their absence in my life.

'You look like a proper gin,' Brenda sometimes told me, or, 'a proper Aboriginal woman.'

The comment made me laugh. I took it as a compliment, although I'm not sure if she meant it that way. Perhaps just an honest observation. I didn't think I was Aboriginal. I didn't feel Aboriginal. In fact, the more time I spent out there immersed in a totally different culture, the more I grew to understand and appreciate my own.

I knew who I was and was contented with that. At the same time, there were things about the *yapa* way of life that suited me well. I liked living outside and being part of the natural environment. I seemed to have a way of going with the flow that fitted in with the *yapa* way. I liked getting dirty and not having to rush off and have a shower or change my clothes, not having to brush my hair on a daily basis, iron my clothes nor operate according to imposed time frames. Out there, people seemed to live in the moment, just being where they were and with who and what they had. There was a lot of laughter and a stoic resourcefulness, going with the flow and making do.

In the summer months at Pulardi, school went from maybe seven in the morning to midday. When the kids seemed to need a break, we'd announce one and go outside for some fresh air and physical activity. Or the kids nicked home and I had a few minutes peace.

By the time the sun had reached its zenith, interest in schoolwork had waned and the room was too hot to stay in, even with the wall slid back. We grabbed something for lunch, perhaps kangaroo and damper again, and some oranges I'd brought from Mount Allan. Everyone piled into the Toyota, a couple riding in the cabin with me and everyone else in the tray back. Brenda or other adults from the community came too. We bounced along dirt tracks to a nearby bore, a few kilometres away. There, a windmill pumped water from underground into a big corrugated-iron tank. In that tank we cooled down, splashing around and playing games. I'd be speaking English, modelling and teaching in an informal setting. I also learnt Anmatyerre from the kids and the adults.

I used to think that those times at the water tank were as educationally valid as anything else I did out there, as well as being at least as productive in terms of race relations and reconciliation.

15

We decided we could do with another staff member at Mount Allan School to do yard work and help look after the kids. School staff included Alastair, Maureen, Maureen's sister Jean, who was employed part-time as a cleaner, and me. Sandy Allan had approached us and expressed an interest. We considered that his presence at the school would be invaluable. We knew we had our full quota of staff from the Education Department, based on attendance numbers. Maybe Sandy could be employed through CDEP. They were always on the lookout for meaningful work to keep the adults of the community employed. This seemed like a perfect opportunity. I drew the short straw and agreed to go and put this request to Janice.

It was a Thursday afternoon, pay day, mail plane day. As I stood at the counter waiting for Janice to finish what she was doing and attend to me, a group of community women entered the office. Most of them were women I knew, whose children came to the school.

'*Nampijinpa*,' one of them greeted me affectionately.

'Hello, my daughter-in-law.'

'Miss Kumenjayi.'

'Hello, sis.'

Janice glanced up whenever anyone acknowledged me in such a way, shot me a glance, then looked back down at her business. 'Linda,' she announced eventually, 'what can I do for you?'

I stepped forward and delivered the pitch I'd been rehearsing, as calmly and respectfully as I could. 'Hi, Janice. We need someone to work at the school to do yard work and help look after the kids. Sandy Allan would like to do it. Could this be a CDEP position?'

'No,' she snapped, then followed up in her officious way. 'It's a school position. The Education Department will have to pay for that.'

'I'm sure there's a way around that,' I replied, trying to contain my emotions. 'How about some flexibility?'

'Don't come in here trying to tell me how to do my job. The rules are that government departments must pay for their own staff. It's in the rules. Is there anything else?'

I bit my tongue and turned to walk away, blinking back tears. I was tired and frustrated. There were so few *kardiya* on that community, trying to do our jobs with a minimum of support or resources. The antagonism was exhausting.

On the way out, I stopped to stand with the community women who were waiting for their pay.

One of the women came up close to me. 'She's rubbish one, this one,' she said to me.

Another of the women added, 'Yeah, she cheeky woman. We don't like her.'

We were talking quietly, huddled together at the back of the office. As was generally the way with the people of Mount Allan, collecting money was a communal affair. I enjoyed being brought into the fold.

One by one, the women were called forward. They tipped their money out of the envelope, counted it, and then signed the register on the counter. Janice seemed to just tolerate this ritual the way she seemed to just tolerate most things.

Sally was called forward. She was the mother of a few schoolkids. She spoke more English than most of the women and had a confidence that stood her apart. She ripped open her envelope and counted her money. 'Where's my other sixty dollars?' she demanded loudly of Janice.

'Max got sixty dollars credit from the store last week for petrol. We took it out of your pay this week to pay the store back. It's community policy now, Sally.'

'What, for someone to pay someone else's debts? Max got credit from the store, take it out of his pay,' Sally snapped.

'He's your husband, isn't he?' Janice continued in her controlled manner.

'He's my fucking husband, he's not me.'

They stood their ground momentarily, Sally raging and Janice cool and composed.

Finally Sally yielded. She threw her pay envelope on the desk. 'Keep your fucking money,' she yelled. 'Shove it up your fucking arse.'

She stormed out of the office and the rest of us followed. Sally cursed and muttered and swore revenge. Eventually, Janice sent a message for Sally to come and get all of her pay. Sally re-entered the office with her group.

'I'll give it to you this time,' Janice told her, 'but if you ever swear at me again, there'll be no more.'

The assembled gathering, me included, stood in anticipation. How would Sally deal with this?

Calmly, she swept her envelope from the counter, signed the register and walked to the door. At the door, she swung around to look straight at Janice and with quiet control she said, 'Fucking white cunt.'

Sally swept out of the office, past a group of assembled men, including Max, who'd been witness to this drama.

'*Warungka*,' the people were calling Janice now, the mad one.

*

Pay brought new clothes, food, toys and petrol. Thirsty cars were fuelled up and people could hit the road: out bush for hunting; to Alice Springs for goods and services; and to other communities to visit relatives.

The other thing that money brought was gambling. After work on pay day, people gathered in big gambling rings, in someone's front yard or in an open, public space. While adults played card games for hours and gambled their weekly earnings, kids wandered.

One of the romantic notions I had when I first got to Mount Allan was that these people were communal and everyone would look after the kids. Alastair said it didn't necessarily work that way and that many kids were neglected while their parents and main caregivers played cards.

I sat down in a gambling ring one afternoon. Cards and money flew in all directions with a logic I couldn't follow.

'You play, Miss Kumenjayi,' people invited me.

I didn't know the rules. I couldn't follow how it worked and it didn't interest me to find out.

When someone had all the money, the game was over. It could take all night and amount to thousands of dollars. Then the winner generally went to town to buy more expensive items that couldn't be afforded with their weekly pay; things like white goods and cars.

'Where's such and such?' you'd ask.

'Oh, he's gone town to buy a car. He won at cards.' That was said matter-of-factly, like of course that's what you would do.

And back he or she would come a few days later, the proud owner of a brand-new second-hand car that ran around for a while and benefitted lots of people.

In that way, gambling was more than just a game. It was a way of pooling money to buy things that people could benefit from. I never found out what happened to people who lost all their money on pay day. I guess others carried them until pay day came around again.

16

'Brian Young's coming,' Maureen told me one morning, grinning widely.

'Who's Brian Young?'

'It's a band, the Brian Young band. You never heard of them? They travel 'round, from Queensland to the west. Everyone loves it when they come.'

'Whitefella?'

'*Yuwayi*, whitefella, but they got *yapa* playing too sometimes.'

For the rest of the week, whenever I went near a community person, they told me, with that same excited tone in their voice, 'Brian Young's coming.' The kids were saying it too.

A new sign was posted outside the shop. 'Brian Young's coming' it read. It was like a new communal mantra. There was a picture of the man himself: wiry and weather-beaten, with an Akubra hat, and big stars adorning his cowboy shirt. Ten dollars for adults and six for children. Thursday 6 June. Sundown.

'Oh, by the way, Brian Young's coming,' Alastair told me one day.

I laughed and told him it was impossible not to know.

'They usually camp at the school,' he said. 'Everyone loves them. It's a bit of fun then they take a whole lot of money out of the community and off they go.'

The Brian Young outback rip-offs, I decided, travelling the country, landing in communities, making their fortune then rambling on. I judged them and put them in the bad guy category.

In they rolled, after school on a pay day, the whole travelling show. There were cars, trucks and vans all emblazoned with the logo. They snaked their way slowly towards us, an entourage of excited kids running along behind them, and pulled up at the school gates.

'Come in, come in,' said Alastair, opening the gates wide.

Suddenly the schoolyard that we'd neatly raked in honour of our important guests became a Brian Young Show parking lot.

Out they stepped: long legs in tight jeans that ended in heeled boots, bodies snug in cowboy shirts, topped off with those outback hats. The men had those older, wizened faces like they'd been travelling the dusty roads, through droughts and flooding rains for a lifetime. The ladies were fresh and slinky, bringing glamour to the outfit. They clearly hadn't caught up with the rule about women dressing to conceal their womanly form or, if they had, they'd chosen not to heed it. Perhaps that was part of the key to their success.

Right out of the poster he stepped and into the school grounds, comfortable and commanding. 'G'day, I'm Brian Young.' He offered around his firm, I'm a decent bloke handshake, first to Alastair then me, then to Maureen and Jean who were waiting in the wings.

I was impressed by the easy respect he showed to the Aboriginal women, treating them no different than he did Alastair or I. He introduced his team – seven men, four women and assorted dogs – and we shook hands all round. One of the pretty women turned out to be Brian Young's wife.

They unpacked and moved on in, just like they owned the school. In came the swags, the tucker boxes and a range of musical instruments. Out came the chocolate biscuits and cigarettes. All of a sudden our humble school caravan was unashamedly transformed from a formal classroom, albeit a van in the middle of the desert, to the dressing room at a gig. The rules went out the window as the entourage boiled the kettle, lit up their smokes and spread out. Kids poked their heads in the door, surveyed the scene and took off as soon as anyone spoke to them.

At six o'clock I was still drinking tea and eating biscuits with various members of the crew and turning a blind eye to them smoking in the classroom. They talked of communities right through, from Queensland to Western Australia. They discussed politics. They related tales, funny and fascinating, of incidents they had encountered and stories they had heard. They spoke with respect for the land and the people of outback Australia.

I found them a bit slick and out for what they could get but they weren't racist and objectionable like Janice or the bloke from the Tilmouth Well Roadhouse. I reserved my mistrust of the Brian Young Band and welcomed their alternative points of view and the variety they offered from the norm, as well as the contribution they made to my growing realisation that it wasn't all black and white, good guys and bad guys, but there were various shades of grey.

As the hours passed, members of the entourage slipped out to our humble ablutions block and emerged more shining and glamorous than ever.

With the sun going down, the community began to arrive. Old people hobbled in on walking sticks or younger people's arms, younger adults came with the babies, youth and children. They brought blankets, admission fees and an air of excitement. They brought extra money, too, for the goodies at the souvenir stall: caps, stickers, T-shirts and cassette tapes all adorned with the brand name.

People paid their fee and shuffled in to claim a spot and set themselves up in front of the temporary stage. With barely a person left back at home, the dogs would be filling the empty air with their mournful howls the way they did when left alone. Alastair came with his family. The other white folk stayed away, with the dogs.

'Ladies and gentlemen, boys and girls, the Brian Young band.'

Hoots from the crowd, spotlights on centre stage and the rootin', tootin', hollerin' show was underway. Songs of love and heartache, people and places, swirling around, uniting us, then wafting out into the desert. Beyond the concentration of lights and noise the sun had set, a soft breeze blew and the moon rose like an illuminated fingernail in the eastern sky.

'My achin' heart, my breakin' heart, a-drovin' the cattle and a-walkin' the dog on the banks of the old Condamine.' The showgirls sang like pretty cockatiels and fooled around with the men on stage, making everybody laugh. They grooved with the kids who'd moved tentatively up the front, drawn by the music and a desire to let their hair down but self-conscious and inhibited. The confidence of the showgirls gave them the encouragement they needed, then everyone laughed at the antics of the kids.

The mood and the easy rocking music got to even me, the cynic from Melbourne who joked about country and western music.

'What do you get if you play a country and western record backwards?'

'You get back your *mayan* (man), your house, your car and your dog.'

It was fresh and fun and a welcome deviation from the norm. I moved up the back to dance in the shadows. Dancing wasn't the done thing. Drinkers danced in town. Women danced at ceremonies. Dancing free-form to modern music was seen as daring and risqué and generally connected to the mating game. Still, music like this got your feet tapping and your body rocking, even if you were sitting down. I got the sense that everyone wanted to dance but generally weren't game. Someone joined me in the dark and then someone else. Women who hadn't danced for years left their husband's sides and slinked over to join us. In clouds of dust that we'd stirred up, with the amplified music booming out across the desert and a skyful of stars twinkling above, we giggled and danced, breaking the rules.

In the morning, too early for most of us to wave them off, the whole Brian Young convoy snaked its way back out of the community the way it had come in.

'Good show, eh?' people said in the days that followed.

'We had a good concert, hey Miss Kumenjayi?'

'We danced, hey Miss Kumenjayi?' with conspirational smiles.

People had less money for essentials that week but we had smiles on our faces, Brian Young paraphernalia and a mojo that lasted long after the dust from the departing convoy had settled.

17

'You talked to Janice?' Maureen asked me.

I told her what had happened in the office, to me and also to Sally.

Maureen nodded. '*Purnku*. Rubbish,' she said quietly.

'Well, why doesn't the community get her to leave and get someone else who likes *yapa* more?'

'Some people wants her here,' Maureen replied. 'And they think if they kick her out they might have to get used to another *warungka*, mad person.'

'Do they think all white women are mad?'

'*Yuwayi*, yes,' she replied, then smiled and added, 'But not you. They think you are *waddara*, not *warungka*.'

We laughed at that. *Waddara* was a person who slept with someone of the wrong skin or just generally slept around. It could be a term of abuse or affection.

'Well, who's gonna pay Sandy?' Maureen asked.

'CDEP is gonna pay him, Maureen. I've just gotta figure out how.'

'Meeting tomorrow,' Maureen dropped in.

'What meeting?'

'Community meeting. The community council have called it.'

'What for?'

'To talk about *Warungka*. She making everyone unhappy, all the whitefellas and the *yapa*. We not having school in the morning. We all gotta go meeting.'

The whole community turned out for the meeting. You could see all the people being drawn in towards the council office: lone cowboys crunching along the gravel road like something out of the wild west; old men and women, some of them frail and ancient-looking; women and kids in chatty groups; husbands and wives with their children. Officials like Janice and Steve and the senior council members were under the veranda. The rest of us spread out onto surrounding grass and dirt. Generally, the men gathered together, standing close to the veranda. The women were further back, seated together on patches of grass. Doro stood with the shop workers, Alastair with his wife.

I took my place, somewhere between the women on the grass and the veranda. The women greeted me the way they did, murmuring my community names. I winked at them, which made everyone smile.

The council president opened the meeting. I strained to hear her introduction.

'We've called this meeting today to try to sort out the problems on this community. We've got troubles here. Mount Allan isn't working together as a community any more. People are fighting and arguing and not working together properly. We've got trouble with the *kardiya*.'

I felt guilty when she said that.

Her husband stepped forward. He was the vice-president. He started off softly but as he went on his voice became increasingly loud and angry until he was yelling and spitting out his words and on the verge of tears. 'You're meant to be here to help us, to work together for the community. Some of you have no shame with what you are doing. You're welcomed into this community and then you start making trouble. I dunno what we gonna do. I want this community to talk today to try and sort it out.'

People murmured and shifted. The opening address had been entirely in English. People spoke amongst themselves briefly then the man who ran the store stepped forward.

'Thank you for this opportunity to speak to the community. We've been having trouble in the store. It's taking a long time to sort our mail. Some of our mail is being opened in the office but it's not the office's business, it's our business.' He turned to look at his wife then, who was standing just behind him.

She stepped forward and confirmed what he'd just said. 'Yes, we feel that Janice is interfering with the way we run the shop. That's not her business. She opens our mail then she comes into the shop and tries to tell us what to do.'

More murmuring and stirring amongst the people.

Doro took her turn and confirmed again what the shop people had said. She kept it brief and was calm and reasonable, citing interference and obstruction from the office.

The whitefellas spoke one at a time with everyone else listening, quietly and politely. In between, the *yapa* spoke in their languages. Sometimes, several *yapa* were speaking at once, apparently all addressing the crowd at the same time. Their words rose up and fell and bounced around all over the place. It appeared unruly and because I couldn't understand what they were saying, I felt an urge to call for law and order and to get on with the meeting. I had to remind myself that the meeting was proceeding and, just because I wasn't in control, it didn't mean it wasn't happening.

At a lull in the conversation, Alastair spoke up and everyone hushed to hear him. 'Good morning, everyone,' he said earnestly, without a hint of the amusement that was his general demeanour. 'We're having trouble at the school too.' He went on to talk about difficulties with getting our mail sorted and about the CDEP issue. He suggested that it was up to the community to decide what they wanted in terms of the work that people did and that the guidelines were very flexible. There were ways around these things, he said, if people were willing to find them. When he had finished, he looked at Ada and then at all the white people. They all nodded.

Janice signalled her intent to speak. She was as neat and composed as ever, articulating her words ridiculously clearly. 'I know that I have upset some people by following the rules. I have to follow those rules as part of my employment here. I don't make them. Governments set them far away from here. I want to see this community running smoothly and properly and following the rules of the country. You people have elected to have CDEP on this community. If you want CDEP, you have to abide by the rules of CDEP. Some people here don't like to do that so they blame me. I'm just doing my job.'

There was a hush and people were looking in my direction. I was the only white person who hadn't yet spoken, except for Steve, who had taken a back seat.

'I've had trouble with Janice too,' I began.

I was conscious of people looking at me. I was conscious of the whole attention of this meeting being turned in my direction. It wasn't something I was used to. Central organising committee yes, spokesperson no.

'People want to work at the school on CDEP. The Education Department won't give us any more money for those positions but we think they are good positions and they would help the school.' I looked at Alastair and he nodded. I seemed to be going all right. Everyone was still listening to me. I continued, calmly, 'The other day when I went into the office to talk to Janice about this…'

I looked at her as I said that. She shot me a stony-faced glance and then threw in a comment. It was barely audible but I caught two little words and the tone I knew only too well: '…the rules.' Those two words; like a red rag to a bull.

I snapped in the way I'd contained in the office, in the way I'd seen Sally do. Suddenly I was yelling at her. 'You and your fucking rules. You make the rules, no one else. You sneak them in then we all get in trouble for not following them. You don't want this community to run well, you just want control.'

Alastair caught my eye and implored me to stop. I wanted to stop and be as rational and calm as all the other *kardiya* but I'd lost control. The dam wall, of pent-up anger and fatigue and frustration, had burst and it all came rushing out.

'Every time I come into that fucking office you make me upset. You don't try to help me or make my job easier for me; you always make it more fucking difficult. You do it to everyone else too with your tight-arse ways and your fucking rules.'

I stopped. I heard stunned silence. People began to talk in their languages again, rapid and noisy. I spoke to no one. I put my head down, turned and walked away, towards school. I choked back tears. In front of the whole community I'd yelled and sworn and made an absolute spectacle of myself while everyone else had calmly told their stories. Maybe they'd ask me to leave now. I wished the red earth beneath my feet would open up and swallow me whole.

Children arrived at school, following me from the meeting. I set up some free activities for them then rejoiced in their company and waited for the other staff to arrive. No one mentioned the meeting or my performance but it hung over me and I waited for the shit to hit the fan.

A community person who I didn't know very well stuck her head inside the classroom door. 'Good job, Miss Kumenjayi,' she said and then she was gone.

Alastair arrived.

I looked at him sheepishly.

'Quite a performance,' he told me.

'What's happened?'

'The council are meeting with Janice and Steve behind closed doors.'

'Am I in trouble?'

He laughed. 'You? You're a star performer! People appreciated what you did.'

In the week that followed, many people came up to me. 'You talked really good,' they told me. 'You're talking for *yapa*.'

I was congratulated everywhere I went.

Sally approached me. 'Good on you,' she said. 'If I was you, I would have hit her over the head.'

That made us both laugh.

The meeting was the talking point of the whole following week. The best news came one evening, a week later, when it came out that Janice was leaving the community but Steve would stay on a bit longer. She'd got enough rope and eventually she'd hung herself.

And Sandy Allan was employed to work at the school on CDEP.

*

As the year went on, Maureen was away from school more often. She was an emerging artist developing a name. She had her contacts from the art world in Alice Springs, where she often went for weekends then increasingly stayed on, painting and promoting her work. She had a boyfriend in town, so that kept her in there too.

Maureen's boyfriend was a white man. She liked the idea of being with a white man, to break away from the oppressive traditions that went with many of the bush relationships. At the same time, she hadn't broken away from the tradition of wanting her man to be initiated. So it was an initiated white man she was after. That greatly reduced the pool she had to choose from. The man she had found who fitted those criteria was nice enough but he was a big drinker and a bit rough around the edges. She disappeared into town for weeks on end with no word then just as suddenly she reappeared and resumed her work at the school.

During my weekends in town, if I knew she was there, I went looking for Maureen. It seemed that if I walked around the central part of town, thinking about her and willing her to appear, she would. It was uncanny how many times that happened. We'd exclaim and embrace then spend some time together and arrange to meet up later. If she was ready at the end of the weekend, Maureen travelled home with me.

One time we'd organised a school sports carnival and schools had come from all around. On the morning of the big event, Maureen was nowhere to be seen and we felt a bit disappointed and let down. This was a big event for our school that Maureen had been involved in planning. About five of our closest schools, some from several hundred kilometres away, were assembled on the grassland by the dam and the sporting events had begun. A car was approaching in the distance. As it came closer, we saw it was a taxi, three hundred kilometres from the nearest rank. It pulled up and out stepped Maureen. She had sold one of her paintings in town to raise the four hundred and fifty dollars for her trip back home.

We relied on Maureen at school and daily teaching was much more difficult without her. Also, without Maureen it was hard to keep in check the doubts about the value or otherwise of the education we were providing. She was great to talk to about it and she believed in what we were doing.

She also offered invaluable support to the students. Without Maureen there, I sometimes felt like an alien, imposing strange and foreign ways that the students couldn't embrace or see as relevant to their lives.

Another community member, Joe Daniels, sometimes filled in as the assistant teacher during Maureen's absences. He wasn't the Joe Daniels Jangala who came to visit me with JB but a different one, a Jampijinba. With the same first and family names, they could be distinguished by their skin names. He cared for the students while they were at school. He looked after their welfare, helped them with their work, interpreted as required and generally provided a positive and supportive presence. It was particularly good to have Joe there, as a local man, to provide encouragement to the young men who struggled with still being at school.

One day after school, Joe had seated himself up at the teacher's desk. He produced a document that he wanted me to read and discuss with him. It was a legal paper, advising him that he had missed a court appearance for a driving offence, and had the option now of going to jail or doing community service.

I dreaded the thought of losing Joe from the school and of him going to jail. 'You can just do community service,' I told him, thinking that was a great option and the solution to the problem. 'You can do it here on the community. You won't have to go away.'

Joe shook his head. 'I like a bit of time in jail,' he told me.

'Why?' I asked, incredulous. I'd never heard of anyone actually wanting to spend time in jail. How could it be a deterrent to committing crime, I wondered, if the inmates wanted to be there?

Joe laughed at the strength of my disbelief. He went on to explain it to me: he'd get three meals a day, a comfortable bed and he'd be able to spend time with lots of family members. Also, he'd be away from the temptation of alcohol.

Later, after Joe had done his jail term, I happened upon him one day in a town camp in Alice Springs. Joe had been drinking and was now sleeping it off, face down in the dirt. I thought back to what he had told me about a comfortable bed courtesy of Her Majesty.

18

The big event on the Western Desert calendar was the Yuendumu sports weekend, held annually over the picnic day long weekend at the beginning of August. It was a huge event that was attended by just about everyone from Mount Allan, without their dogs, who were left behind to howl.

Mount Allan fielded two main teams: the women's softball and the men's Aussie rules football. Festivities started on the Friday and Warriyi-Warriyi was practically empty by the time I left on Saturday morning.

Yuendumu was abuzz with thousands of people who travelled from right across the central desert and beyond to attend this annual gathering.

I had just driven in when I came upon Maureen. She was sitting by the side of a main Yuendumu thoroughfare. I stopped the car and as I went to her I realised she looked messy; she was slumped, her hair was all matted and what was holding it in clumps was blood. Maureen was bleeding from her head.

'They hit me,' she told me simply.

'Who hit you?' I demanded.

'My husband's sisters and his aunties.'

I was outraged and confused. I wanted to run after them and hit them back. I wanted to turn them over to the police. It turned out to be part of what was called 'finishing up business', following the death of someone's spouse. Maureen had started seeing someone new without waiting the requisite amount of time or getting permission from her deceased husband's family. Her penalty for this was to be hit over the head with a nulla nulla: a wooden stick, about a metre and half long, carved from desert hardwood. It could be used for digging in the earth, for fighting or meting out punishments. After thumping her and making her head bleed, they told her it was okay, she was free to go and be with someone else.

I had to fight back tears. After all she'd gone through with her mean, drunken husband, she now had to suffer this. Some of the bush ways seemed so irrational and unfair. I'd seen those women play softball too. I knew how hard they flogged the ball. I couldn't imagine the headache that would result from taking a blow like that. I scooped Maureen up and took her to my friend's house, where she was able to shower and clean up. She went off then, with family.

Yuendumu was pumping. It felt like the entire population of the central desert communities had descended here for the weekend. There was the customary chaos of blackfellas en masse: laughter, screeching, yelling, babies crying, hordes of people moving around, food, disorder, rubbish. I was walking down the main street, a solo whitefella moving comfortably amidst the throngs. Occasionally I saw someone I knew, mostly people from Yuendumu or Mount Allan or someone I recognised from Alice Springs. There was a smattering of non-Aboriginal people and we tended to know each other or of each other. We acknowledged one another and often kept going unless we were actually friends. I enjoyed being in this setting and moving easily amongst the desert people. I didn't feel like an outsider. I just felt like a person amongst people, doing their thing and getting along.

I bumped into some of the Pulardi, mob who piled into my car and got a lift with me back to their camp. It was in the bush on the outskirts of Yuendumu, in the direction of Pulardi. I realised that's generally what the visiting bush people did: they set up camp in the bush in the direction from which they came.

The camp was in a clearing in the bush. It was set up to accommodate about twenty people, divided into small family groups who each had their own windbreak with a campfire and a few swags around each. The windbreaks were much like the one at my home made of car bonnets, just a few feet high, but in this instance they were made of tree branches that had been artfully woven together to build resilient structures. The earth in the whole area had been swept clean, probably with branches that served effectively as bush brooms. The Pulardi mob had arrived on Friday and after one night of camping had settled right in.

'Here, Miss Kumenjayi, you sleep with us,' Cameron told me.

I put my rolled up canvas swag down where he indicated.

'Mum's at the football,' he told me.

'Will we go there?'

'Yep.'

The footy ground was red dust bordered by a white pole fence. A crowd was gathered on the fence, all around the ground; in cars, on chairs they'd brought along, on blankets or standing. A match was in progress on the gravelly, dusty bare ground. While the players all sported the footy jumper and matching shorts of their team that kept them uniform in some way, they were a variety of shapes and sizes, from skinny athletic beanpoles to round, puffing bags of wind. This incongruous look was exacerbated by the range of accessories that the players did or didn't wear: some wore beanies, some wore footy boots, some were in runners and several of the players were running around and kicking the ball in bare feet.

The sky was sheer blue and the sun beat down with an intensity that could still burn, even though a chill wind blew across the open plain.

Brenda smiled when she saw Cameron and me approaching and shuffled over to make room for us to stand with her, next to the fence.

'How come they play with no shoes?' I asked.

Brenda shrugged and smiled. 'Couldn't find their boots?' she replied.

'Doesn't it hurt their feet?'

'You know how blackfellas are,' she told me. 'We tough.'

We laughed.

'Did you play softball?' I asked.

'*Yuwayi*, Mount Allan won two games. We in the finals now, tomorrow. You gotta come and watch.'

'I'll be there,' I told her.

That evening we went to the battle of the bands. Contenders from across the region appeared on the stage beside the main store to strut their stuff. The music had the country rock flavour that was quintessentially Aboriginal and Central Australian. Hordes sheltered together against the biting winds to witness this Eurovision of the Western Desert. Food stalls had been set up by enterprising local groups to cash in on the huge crowds of hungry people who would rather eat out and be amongst the action than stay back at their camps and cook. Some of the stalls were barbecues that had been carved out of forty-four-gallon drums. Huddled up to them you could score a chewy steak sandwich along with warmth from the open fire.

Back at the camp, Stephanie snuggled in with me that night and we did our usual rendition of 'Twinkle Twinkle Little Star' before falling asleep beneath a sky filled with them.

Next morning after a breakfast of tea and damper, we descended en masse again, filling the streets and buildings of Yuendumu and stretching its resources to the limit. Food, toilets, petrol, drinks: the demands of thousands of bush visitors were enormous.

Mount Allan did well in the softball finals but went down by a few runs to Papunya. The women had an amazing swinging action that thwacked the ball and sent it flying long distances. The football competition continued until only the very best were left standing. There were also more traditional activities like corroborree dancing and spear throwing.

I wandered around Yuendumu for that day and the next, meeting up with people and accompanying them to the various events, dirty, crumpled and often with one or another snotty-nosed, cheeky, adorable infant on my hip.

The footy was meant to finish on Monday afternoon but games had been delayed so it was announced that the grand final would spill over onto Tuesday. I was ready for a shower and clean clothes by then and I thought I'd better turn up for school in case any of the kids did. Mostly they would stay, along with their families, until the grand final footy game was over.

The Yuendumu sports weekend was an important cultural and social event on the Western Desert calendar. It brought families and communities together and was owned and run by and for local people. It was also a great weekend away that we talked about and wrote about in school for many weeks after.

*

Towards the end of the year, Teddy Briscoe asked me what I was doing for Christmas. He invited me to stay at Pulardi and have kangaroo and VB in the river. Tempting as that sounded, and as close to an Aussie Christmas as one could get, I declined and headed back down south for my annual catch up with family and friends.

19

I returned to Mount Allan in 1991 as the head teacher. Alastair had decided to move on with his family. I applied for and was granted his position. My only reluctance was it meant relinquishing my position at Pulardi.

I got back to find that Alastair's demountable van, which I was now moving into, had been broken into and trashed during the summer holidays. The community people blamed outsiders: petrol sniffers from the nearby community of Papunya. It was a scourge affecting Aboriginal populations in Central Australia: young people getting hold of petrol and sniffing it in order to get high. They tended to syphon it out of cars and carry it around in tin cans that they held up to their faces. It was a terrible pursuit that did untold damage to bodies and minds and led to horrendous behaviour. It also broke families' hearts and tore communities apart. Mount Allan didn't have a problem with petrol sniffing, unlike some of its nearest neighbours.

The Education Department were to send out workers to repair my demountable. In the meantime, the CDEP coordinator's house was vacant so I could stay there. It was early in the new year and school hadn't yet started. The house was a three-bedroom brick veneer, recently vacated by Janice and Steve. It was a standard, suburban kind of dwelling with security doors and screens. There was a house next door occupied by some other white workers. I knew them to say hello to.

One evening, I heard a knocking at the door. 'Who's there?'

A muttered name. 'Let me in.'

I didn't know the man. 'What do you want?'

'I want you, let me in.'

'No,' I replied. 'Go away.'

He wouldn't go away. He spent hours trying to get through the security and get at me. I called out but the neighbours didn't hear. I kept telling him to go away but he wouldn't listen. I was completely isolated. I had no way of contacting anyone and just some structural security that I hoped would be strong enough to stand between this man and the horror of what he wanted to inflict on me. I was terrified.

The structural security did hold up. After what seemed like an eternity, he went away. When I was sure he was gone, I fled next door. They comforted me and put me up for the rest of the night. It turned out that the man came and went from Mount Allan and he wasn't quite right in the head.

*

Amanda McMahon transferred over from Hermannsburg to work with me. She took my former position as the visiting outstation teacher at Pulardi, working part-time at Mount Allan. We were excited about working together. She was young and fresh and had great teaching ideas. Amanda came with her partner Jack, who was a union worker and a decent, committed bloke.

During the summer break, the demountable that was to be Amanda and Jack's home had been trashed. Petrol sniffers had done it, the community told us; out-of-towners who'd drifted in during the summer break.

*

It was a Saturday night in February, my first trip to Alice Springs for 1991. Maureen and I were, as she laughingly observed, 'Two *kungkas*, Aboriginal women, out on the town.' Maureen was spending most of her time in Alice Springs by then and I missed her. Earlier that day, in the centre of town, I wandered around town calling her to me then I turned a corner and there she was; the telepathic link-up.

The day had cooled down to a manageable level. That's what happened during the summer months. The days were so extremely hot that you had to stay indoors in the air conditioning. After sunset and as the dark descended, we could emerge like nocturnal creatures to get lively in the cooler hours. To step out, we dressed up in our own Central Australian fashion; shorter skirts and prettier tops than we dared during the day.

Maureen and I decided to go out to the Pioneer Club. Pioneers were one of the town football teams, made up largely of Aboriginal players who lived in Alice Springs. Their clubroom was a tin shed on the banks of the river to the north of town where they often hosted parties on a Saturday night.

Inside, a band played country rock. In the low light, between the band at one end and the bar at the other, people moved to the music. They spilt out too, onto the grounds outside, with their beers and dramas and love affairs. Most were Aboriginal but there was a smattering of white folk; community workers and schoolteachers and the like who preferred the mixed socialising.

I was at the bar buying a drink.

'Allo,' said the man next to me, with a handsome smile and a swagger of confidence.

'Hello,' I replied and we clinked glasses.

'Where you from?' The standard question.

'I'm from Melbourne but now I live at Mount Allan.'

'Ah Warriyi-Warriyi.' He paused as if to digest that, then asked, '*Kultitja?*'

'Yep,' I nodded and he nodded too, as though whatever he'd heard was now falling into place.

Sometimes it seemed like nothing could happen in the Western Desert without everyone knowing about it. Or maybe it was just the convivial way those people had, of making you feel like you mattered.

I grinned to myself about the *Kultitja* word and how far I had come since I first heard it. I had barely met an Aboriginal person back then, especially one from the bush, and I didn't know how to talk to them. Here

I was now, out with my *yapa* sister, clinking glasses with a local man in a room filled with Aboriginal people, feeling comfortable and welcome.

'Where are you from?'

'From Sydney,' he replied and laughed, so pleased with his little joke that I laughed along with him. With his broad facial features and deep brown skin, he was clearly a central desert man. 'Nah, I'm from up the road. *Warlpiri* country. A little outstation called Central Bore. You know it?'

I shook my head.

'It's not on most of the maps,' he told me. 'It's just a little place where my family comes from. Our little resort.'

'I bet it's lovely.'

'Yeah, it's lubly, but a bit quiet for me. I prefer to stay in town these days. I just go back to visit sometimes... I play in a band. The Spinifex Rats. You heard of us?'

I told him I hadn't.

'I'd like to play a song for you sometime.'

I told him my name then, yelling for him to hear me over guitar riffs and the beat of drums.

Scotty was his name. He was like someone from the bush with that Aboriginal English way of talking. At the same time, he seemed more urbane than the desert men I had come to know. He had a sweet, soft voice and an affable way that kept me standing there, beside the bar, turned partially towards him and partially to the crowd.

Scotty had never been to Melbourne, he told me, but he'd really like to go. 'I like the city,' he told me, shaking his head with a faraway look, like he had transported himself there. 'Too many people, too many opportunities.' He didn't mean 'too many' in my way of using the expression. He meant too many in the Central Australian Aboriginal way, as in a thrilling amount. His excitement was infectious.

Maureen had wandered off but now she reappeared and she and Scotty acknowledged one another. I turned to talk to her and Scotty turned to talk to someone else.

'Leave him,' she whispered to me. 'He's trouble.'

But it was too late. The attraction had already begun and, trouble or not, I was in. I was an experiential learner with a stubborn tendency to dive into currents, the stronger the better, then swim like crazy.

Scotty and I left the dance together. I had some swags in the back of the car and we went and camped near a bridge, in the bush to the north of town. We drank a few more beers and got amorous. I enjoyed his curiosity and intelligence, his sense of fun and his warm brown skin.

In the morning, I dropped Scotty home. Several people were sitting around out the front of the house, watching in their surreptitious way, as we pulled up. Scotty squeezed my hand on the gearstick as he got out of the car.

*

February drifted on. It was the hottest month and any refreshment I had brought back from my southern break was long dissipated. It was hot and sticky all day and all night and although the summer rains were needed there were none in sight.

*

Amanda was travelling out to Pulardi three days a week and developing her own relationship with the Pulardi mob. I stayed put in my new capacity, running things at Mount Allan School. For the other two days, or more if the Pulardi schoolkids weren't home, Amanda worked with me as I had done with Alastair. She brought new energy to school practices. She also challenged some of the old order that had been established over the years that I had just gone along with.

There was a girl in the community called Cindy. People called her the mad one. She was intellectually disabled. Cindy was cared for by her family. She was about fourteen years of age but her intellectual age was much lower and she had never been to school. During the day she drifted around, engaging where she could. That's the way it was when I turned up and one of the many things I just went along with.

Amanda disagreed with Cindy's lack of schooling. She arranged to have her tested by Education Department specialists. Through this, Cindy's special needs were diagnosed and funding was made available. We were then able to employ a community person to attend school with Cindy and support her in the classroom. Cindy loved coming to school with all the other young folk. It was a credit to Amanda that she addressed that situation and an indictment on the rest of us.

*

I didn't give Scotty a lot of thought. As is generally the way out bush, you live in the moment, in the situations as they turn up. Scotty was a nice recent memory for me and someone I might bump into again one day.

A few weeks down the track, I went on one of my outings to Yuendumu. I was on my way home, on the outskirts of the community, when he turned up, like an apparition, strolling along the side of the road. My heart skipped a beat and I pulled up beside him. He opened the passenger door and poked his head in.

'Hello,' I said to him.

'Allo.' Ah, that sweet, high voice, that accent and his handsome smile. He seemed a bit more reserved now, perhaps without the alcohol. 'Where you going?'

'Sydney,' I told him and we laughed. 'Where are you going?'

'I came to Yuendumu for band meeting. Finished now. I'm just going for walk.'

We sat there in a loaded silence which he finally punctuated with what I guess we both were thinking. 'You want a passenger for Sydney?'

It felt reckless and scary but there was me, a bold outback girl always up for an adventure. 'Come on then, jump in,' I replied so he did, like that was the most normal thing in the world. Like a Western Desert hunter and musician could jump into the work vehicle of a southern teacher passing through without telling anyone where he was going, like it was prearranged that I would pick him up on the road out of Yuendumu at 5.48 or whatever time it was and he would come with me to Mount Allan. If not prearranged then preordained, and that is how it felt.

Scotty stayed with me that night. He stayed the next. He stayed for several nights. And then he just stayed on. He'd moved in, I suppose, as simple as that. Marriage, bush style! I enjoyed his company and this newfound intimacy. Amanda had a partner. Just about everyone around me had a partner. Now I had one too.

Nothing went unnoticed at Mount Allan.

'You got husband, hey, Miss Kumenjayi?'

Or 'You got wipe [wife]?' the kids said to me.

I think the community took it in their stride. Their lives were so family-oriented that this new rainbow alliance between their head teacher and a bloke from the bush probably made at least as much sense to them as me living alone.

During the day, I went off to school to do my job. At lunchtime, I went home to use the radio telephone. Scotty might be there milling about or off with people he knew. He had relations at Mount Allan and seemed to fit in comfortably. In the afternoons, I returned home but no longer to my own quiet space. Scotty dusted off my guitar and gave it new life. More visitors than ever came over now and we sang and talked and drank cups of tea into the evening.

Scotty and I were just as happy to be alone together. We talked a lot. We wrote new songs, then sang them and tweaked them. Scotty had a soft, slightly high voice that I found endearing. His words were tinged with the local accent. He sang songs in pidgin English too, to make me laugh.

It was simple and peaceful. We enjoyed each other's company. We delighted in our cultural differences and learning from each other. I showed Scotty how to cook some of the things I made that he most liked to eat: shepherd's pie, tuna curry, lasagne. He liked the way I kept the house clean and in order. He marvelled at the way I could artfully stack a mountain of dishes into the dish drainer without any of them crashing down.

I marvelled at things about Scotty. He could hear a song on the radio once then play it on the guitar. He crafted beautiful drawings without any awareness of the talent that he had. One afternoon, I brought home a packet of sixteen thick coloured markers and some art paper. I returned home at lunchtime the next day to find Scotty putting the finishing touches to a colourful, vibrant bush scene, done in pop-art style.

My praises encouraged Scotty and soon after that he came to school one afternoon to head up an art lesson. The kids responded as positively to Scotty as they did to any Aboriginal teachers in the school. Absorbed in their own artistic creations, they giggled and gossiped away in their languages about Scotty being my husband. I got the gist of what they were saying.

Scotty enjoyed his afternoon in the school. 'They should come and help you,' he told me, referring to the community and my need for a regular assistant teacher. Maureen still came and went, as did Joe Daniels.

Some afternoons, we went walking. Scotty generally wore shoes but it didn't seem to bother him if he didn't. The bottoms of his feet were like leather that prickles couldn't penetrate. In the way of a bush hunter, Scotty's senses were tuned to this environment he knew so well.

In the bush, Scotty taught me the names of more plants and birds. He could read and write Warlpiri, so he knew how to spell words that I might have been taught before but they were confirmed for me now by spelling them. He took me to distant waterholes of cool, pure water that we drank, in the way of his ancestors, by lying on our bellies and lapping it up with our tongues or cupping it in our hands. He taught me how to read the ground for animal tracks and how you could follow those to hunt the animal. He could read weather patterns and weather conditions too.

'Is it going to rain?' I asked him, and 'What will the weather be like tomorrow?' It was like having my own weather man on tap.

Scotty held his knowledge of the bush not in an academic way but in a way that no amount of study could achieve; an intrinsic way of knowing that went right to his core.

A while later, when I took Scotty to Melbourne, he applied those same skills in the city. He read every street sign, every billboard and every piece of public writing as though his very life depended on it. It drove me crazy in the city, how long it took us to get from A to B and how very interested he was in every single little thing. It seemed to me that same level of heightened observation that served you well as a hunter in the desert could eventually drive you quite crazy in the city.

For me, our relationship was like an extension of the connections I'd been developing with the people out bush; in some ways a logical next step. Also, I'd been feeling like a fish out of water living alone in a place where family meant the world to everyone around me. Being with Scotty filled the gap and gave me an increased sense of belonging.

20

One day, Scotty announced he would like to take my car to the outstation to visit his family and join in on a card game. I agreed. I didn't need the car. I was glad to get some time back for myself and I knew he was a bit bored at Mount Allan with me at work all day. He came back a few days later. These trips away became regular.

Next he started to take my car and go to Alice Springs. He needed to go in for recording, he told me, or to visit people. That was okay. He looked after my car and he was always back soon enough. There was a simple way out there of living in the moment. Without much access to telephones or other immediate forms of communication and with the long distances people travelled, you often didn't know who would be turning up or when. You just lived with the people around you and when others turned up you lived with them too.

Also, with Scotty away, some of my original visitors, like JB and Joe, were free to come and visit. It didn't seem so suitable for my gentlemen callers to visit me now that I had a live-in boyfriend.

'I've missed you,' he'd say when he returned. And 'You're my woman.' And 'Have you been seeing anyone else while I've been gone?'

'No, Scotty, I only want to be with you.' It seemed boring and silly but sometimes I'd have to go to great lengths to assure him before he'd drop the subject.

*

Scotty and I decided to head to Alice Springs together for the Easter of 1991. I looked forward, with some trepidation, to emerging from the cocoon we'd spun at Mount Allan. Out bush we were okay, with the ways of being and doing that operated there. How would this translate to town where I had all my friends and I operated according to different cultural norms that were much more in line with the way I had grown up?

We set off on the Friday afternoon, after school. Scotty drove. I enjoyed relinquishing control of the wheel and cruising along in the passenger seat for a change. I felt safe with Scotty driving. He'd grown up travelling these roads. He took it easy, guiding the car gently over potholes and other patches of rough road. He always seemed tuned in to the road ahead. You had to be on those roads, always on the lookout for cattle or kangaroos or other unexpected conditions.

Scotty finished a can of soft drink and threw the empty onto the back seat.

'Aren't you going to throw it out the window?' I asked tongue-in-cheek. Everyone else from out that way seemed to just throw their rubbish out the window.

'No,' he replied with a vehemence that took me by surprise. 'Lizards crawl in through the hole at the top and then they can't get out. They get trapped in there and die.'

I'd never before heard Scotty express environmental principles. He knew the bush like the back of his hand but environmentalism wasn't generally something he practised consciously. I was an environmentalist from the suburbs and being with a man who knew the land intrinsically and had a sense of belonging to it was part of his appeal for me. Perhaps part of the appeal for him of being with me was having greater access to suburban comforts, including those I would have liked to leave behind.

We arrived in town after dark. I directed Scotty to the share house I stayed in and he pulled up out the front.

'See you, babe,' he said to me.

'Don't you want to come in? Say hello to my friends?' I would have liked to introduce Scotty around, show him off and see how he went socialising with my mob.

'Nah, you go in. I'll come back later and find you.'

'When?' I asked, keen to understand how our relationship was going to work in town.

He shrugged. 'Might be tomorrow.'

I watched him walk off into the river.

I was sleeping outside in a swag, nestled into an alcove against the side of the house.

That night I had a dream. I was in a place, like a warehouse that was filled, room after room, with racks of thick, dusty coats. A man was chasing me and, as I fled from one room to the next, I had to push through these dense rows of coats that were slowing me down. I was terrified and woke in the dark to find Scotty standing over me.

'Who was that man?' he asked and I realised he was quite drunk.

I snapped quickly out of my sleep. 'Which man?'

'That man I just saw leaving.' He sounded angry and threatening.

I sensed that I was in danger and attempted to appease him. 'There was no man, Scotty. I've been asleep. Come on, get in here and go to sleep.'

It took a bit of convincing but Scotty eventually acquiesced, crawled in beside me and promptly fell asleep.

We woke with the rising sun. Scotty took off, telling me he'd be back later. I got on with my Easter break with friends in town, the other part of my life.

I didn't see Scotty again until mid-Sunday morning when he turned up again, this time calling to me from out the front. He was dishevelled and dirty and the smell of stale alcohol suggested he had been drinking quite heavily.

I approached him casually, taking it in my stride. 'Hi, Scotty.'

'Who've you been with?' he demanded angrily.

'My friends,' I replied innocently, like this was a normal question that I was obliged to answer.

'Nah, who've you been sleeping with?'

'I've been sleeping by myself, out the back. You know…'

Suddenly, out of nowhere and quick as a flash Scotty's clenched fist connected with my jaw. He punched me. I think the shock of that more than the physical force knocked me to the ground. I sat, looking up at him, feeling small and shocked. Being hit by your lover, 'your man', it wasn't something I had grown up with, not something that was anywhere close to my reality. It was, until that moment, something that happened to other people.

Gerard, a friend of mine who lived in the house, came out towards us. 'Are you okay?' he asked me. He must have known what happened.

I told him I was okay and I didn't need any help. The truth was I really wasn't okay and I desperately did need help but I was frightened and stunned and I didn't know how to say that. Gerard went back inside.

Scotty barked orders at me which I obeyed like a dog. I drove the car around town with him beside me in the passenger street, telling me where to drive. I was tempted to disobey his orders and drive to the police station but again I was too frightened. Scotty told me he was looking forward to later in the day when the bottle shop would open and he could buy some more grog. He was angry and volatile and I spent my time obeying and working at appeasing him. I hoped and prayed that he was wrong about the bottle shop and it wouldn't open on Easter Sunday. The hours that alcohol can be sold in Alice Springs are quite restricted. The single most important thing as far as I could see was that no more grog would be involved.

We were crossing the river at the causeway near St Phillips just to the north of town. Scotty reached into the back of the car and produced a hunting rifle he'd tucked in behind the seat. I hadn't known until then that it was there. He fired a shot out his side window, right behind a cyclist who was riding over the river in the same direction as us.

I sometimes wonder about that cyclist, whether he shat himself and thought he'd been shot as the bullet whizzed past.

'I'll use it on you too,' he slurred.

I pulled up, as instructed, in an open area on the outskirts of town where a communal game of cards was underway. A large group was seated in a circle. Others spilled out, around the circle, looking bedraggled and sucking on beers or casks of cheap wine left over from the night before. Scotty got out of the car while I stayed in the driver's seat. One of Scotty's mates walked towards us, a heavy drinker and one of very few bush people who I ever found to be nasty and unpleasant. Could I drive off right then and leave Scotty behind? I contemplated it briefly then thought about the volatile state he was in and that rifle behind the back seat. The consequences of not making it out were too serious.

'I just hit her,' Scotty said to his mate.

'You're mad,' his mate said in reply.

We left them and drove around some more. Scotty was still barking orders and I remained frightened and compliant.

'Let's just go back out bush,' I urged every now and again, ever so gently.

Eventually Scotty agreed.

I drove out of town and turned onto the Tanami Highway for the long drive back to Mount Allan. It was Easter Sunday afternoon. I was resentful that my Easter break in town had been cut short and ashamed that I, in my teaching position of responsibility and trust, found myself in this situation. Along that long lonely desert highway, Scotty fell asleep, a foul, wine-soaked, fleshy blob, slumped against the passenger door. He disgusted me. I pondered whether I could lean over, open the door and push him out without him waking up. I figured if I failed he'd hurt me and that threat was what seemed to hold me back.

Mount Allan was deserted when we got back, except for lonely, howling dogs. Almost everyone had gone away for Easter.

Next morning, Scotty and I talked about what had happened. He told me he was sorry, he didn't want to lose me and he wouldn't do it again.

*

Life resumed in the cocoon with me working all day then coming home to keep Scotty company and cook his dinner. We still had the music, the visitors and okay times. Scotty often took the car and went on his excursions to Central Bore or Alice Springs. It was only when I was diagnosed with sexually transmitted infections that I realised he was sleeping with other women during his sojourns.

'I'm sorry,' he said. 'I won't do it again,' and 'Don't leave me.'

I wanted to go back to my other life at Warriyi-Warriyi, focussing on my teaching and my friendships. The periods of loneliness I'd experienced back then seemed desirable now, at least more so than the loneliness and drama of being in an abusive relationship. I wanted Scotty out of my life but I didn't know how to achieve that without him hurting me.

A couple of times when I went anywhere near suggesting we break up, he'd ask me, 'Do you want to leave me?' There was a threat in his way of asking. I knew that fist was clenching at his side.

'No,' I'd reply as convincingly as I could manage.

It occurred to me that I'd lived a carefree life until then. Whatever choices I'd made, whatever situations I had gotten myself into, I'd always been able to turn around at will. Any relationships I'd been in, if I wanted out, or he wanted out, we'd talk and listen to each other and make mutually respectful decisions. Now, for the first time in my life, I felt like I'd dealt myself a hand I wasn't free to just play the way I chose.

Instead, I engaged in a careful game of charades, never letting on that I wanted out, until I could figure out how to achieve it. I thought about asking the community for help but I didn't know whose side they would be on. Scotty was related to those people, some more closely than others. They had enough problems of their own and one of them was domestic violence. How sympathetic would they be? Also, I was meant to be there to help, not to add my own burdens.

It wasn't all awful. I liked Scotty and enjoyed his company. In the careful act of playing charades, sometimes I forgot that I was playing and often we had really nice times. Maybe it will be okay, maybe he won't do those things again, maybe it's not so bad after all, I'd think to myself. Then caution and sense would take hold: he hit you. He sleeps with other women. They always do it again. Those things are unacceptable for you in your life. Get away.

The internal tug-of-war continued as the orange hues of the autumnal months washed across the desert.

*

Not long after Easter, Teddy Briscoe had a stroke. He was in hospital in Alice Springs and it was said that he might not recover. I was as shaken by this as everyone else. JB came to me and asked me to take him into town on the weekend to see his father. I agreed. My good friend Cath D was up visiting from Melbourne, so she would come too. Scotty and Baby Blue decided to come along for the ride. We dropped them at a popular watering hole to the north of town and left Cath to explore Alice Springs.

Johnny and I went to visit Teddy. We found him in a ward on the third floor, sitting in a wheelchair in a blue hospital gown. It was so good to see this beautiful and familiar man who we loved but it was disturbing too. Teddy's cotton gown had come open at the front and he was wearing nothing underneath, so his nakedness was fully exposed. His whole left side was paralysed. He tried to speak but what came out was a mass of slurring that I could make no sense of. From that powerful, eloquent man who sat, holding court, on his bush community, it broke my heart to see Teddy like this. Johnny also seemed at a loss. I held Teddy's hand and told him I loved him. We stayed for about an hour. On the way to the ground floor, I cried in the elevator with Johnny helpless beside me.

We picked up Cath and then our other two passengers on the way out of town. They took my keys to put something in the boot of the car. I knew they'd been drinking and I suppose I knew at some level what they were putting in the boot. Preoccupied as I was with Teddy, I didn't think clearly about what they were doing. I was wary of Scotty too, particularly because he was charged up and I wanted to avoid the drama of challenging him.

We were heading along the Tanami Highway on the way back home. It was the time of day known in Warlpiri as *uraji*, late afternoon, when the sun is low in the western sky, casting a golden glow across the land. It's exactly the wrong time to drive due west along the Tanami, straight into the sun's blinding rays. And it's exactly, exactly the wrong time to be driving due west along the Tanami when you've never driven on that road before.

Nevertheless, Cath was driving. I'm not sure why. We were up to the long unmade, corrugated section of the road, not far off the bitumen when…smash. The front end of my old blue Holden collided with the rear end of a bush cow, a great solid beast that was standing in the middle of the road. The car thumped to a halt and the passengers along with it. The front end was crumpled and water started spewing out from under the bonnet. The beast staggered off into the scrubland and collapsed.

None of us was injured; shocked perhaps, but physically intact. When your car breaks down on the Tanami Highway, you don't call roadside service. You don't call anyone. You can't. You use your resources. You figure it out. You get the car going and if you can't do that you leave it behind and jump in with someone else.

JB started working on the front of the car. He took off the crumpled bonnet and threw it into the bush by the side of the road. The grill at the front of the radiator had been smashed and water was leaking out. JB started to pinch each bar of the grill back together. It was a long, tedious job and he worked way into the night.

The cow moaned until it died and Baby Blue followed it into the bush and sliced a hunk of meat off its rump. 'That's mine,' he told us all in his drunken state as he put it on the dashboard. 'No one else can have that.'

It was certainly safe from Cath and me, and the others didn't show much interest either.

We snatched bits of sleep, huddled together on the bench seats of the car.

In the morning, we started up the car and limped back home to Mount Allan with Baby Blue protecting his hunk of rump all the way. JB's radiator repair held out, as did the shirt he shoved into the top of the radiator in place of a cap. It took many hours to limp the two hundred kilometres, stopping at every bore and dam to top up the radiator with muddy water.

Back home, Baby Blue took the supplies from the boot and disappeared into the community.

The next day, I was summoned to a council meeting. Someone brought a load of grog into the community, I was told, people got drunk and there was trouble. It came in my car and therefore I was responsible.

I was shattered and felt so ashamed. 'I didn't bring the alcohol,' I said in my defence. 'Those two other men brought it in.'

Perhaps I could have stopped them. I don't know. I hadn't tried. I could see how this looked from the community's point of view and I knew they were thinking about asking me to leave.

'He's living with me and I don't know what to do about it.' That was as close as I went to asking the community for help. 'I love this community. I love living here and I love your kids. I wouldn't do anything to make trouble.'

They talked amongst themselves in language while I stood there, patiently awaiting my fate, feeling utterly lost and ashamed.

Finally it was announced that a decision had been reached. 'It's all right, Miss Kumenjayi. You can stay. We know you love our kids. But don't ever let this happen again.'

I thanked them and gave a heartfelt assurance that it wouldn't.

*

The weeks went by and it was like I was living in a holding pattern. I decided I was too far out. I needed the kind of support my society could offer. Reluctantly, I announced that at the end of the semester, halfway through the year, I would leave my position at Mount Allan. It broke my heart but I couldn't go on living like this and it seemed like the best course of action.

Amanda and Jack decided they would leave too. They'd done a great job in the time they'd been there and fallen in love with the community and school the way I had, but the turbulence of my life had affected them as well.

In the days leading up to my leaving, I recorded the kids reading storybooks and singing. I needed to capture their dear voices exuding their trademark love and enthusiasm. We recorded on audio cassettes in those days.

I told them I was leaving and they would be getting new teachers.

'But why,' they asked me. 'What's wrong?'

'I'm tired. I need to go back to my family,' I told them.

On other occasions someone would repeat it back to me. 'You're tired, hey, Miss Kumenjayi? You need to go back to your family?'

I nodded and hugged them to me. They were loyal and faithful and seemed to take it all in their stride.

Leaving the community was sad. We hugged and cried and I felt like I left a part of myself behind. Later, someone told me that the first community you lived in would always be the one you loved the most. Like your first love.

I've never really gotten over leaving Mount Allan and the circumstances under which I did. It had been such a special time and I left before I was ready.

Sally's husband Max came up and shook my hand. 'How long have you been here?' he asked me. 'Five years?'

It had only been just over eighteen months but I appreciated his perspective. Calling it a year and a half didn't seem to do justice to the magnitude of my experience there.

I left Mount Allan and headed for Pulardi. Teddy's recovery had surpassed anyone's expectations. He was back sitting cross-legged on his swag beneath the cedar tree.

'Miss Kumenjayi. We get you a caravan and you can stop here at Pulardi.'

I declined his generous offer. I needed to get back to my own people.

I hit the Tanami Highway heading for Alice Springs. It was mid-afternoon and the sun shone in the back window. Dust poured out behind as I drove the road which I knew now almost like the back of my hand, right down to the stand of trees beside which my old blue car bonnet lay rusting.

It was a cool winter's day. Still, the sky was perfect blue and the sun shone brightly. It was ideal driving weather. I carried with me some domestic essentials: a swag, a billycan, cups and saucers. I had fewer possessions with me now than I'd had on my way out, having shed some along the way. But I'd gained too: photographs that told a pictorial story of my time at Mount Allan; a cassette recording of precious school moments; some local paintings; a man who would soon be following me into town.

I thudded off the dirt and hit the bitumen at the interface between one world and the other.

21

Scotty walked up to me in the Todd Mall, amidst the ornamental grapevines growing over lattice work and people meandering about their business. I'd been doing that too until he stood there in front of me, with hope written all over his dear, familiar face.

I hadn't seen him for the month I'd been living in Alice Springs. I was renting a room in a friend's house, working as a teacher and trying to get my life back in order. My heart leapt when I saw him; I was thrilled and terrified in equal measure. On one hand, he was lovable and funny and so damn pleased to see me. On the other hand, these feelings I had for him weren't helpful in my bid to be free. I was terrified, not because of what he might do to me, out there amongst the business people and tourists on the streets of Alice Springs, but because of what I might do, the tendency I had to break my resolve and let him back in.

'Allo,' he said, standing there almost sheepishly, like butter wouldn't melt in his mouth. ''Ow are you?' That high-pitched, endearing voice.

'I'm okay.' Standing firm. He seemed so sweet and familiar.

'I've missed you,' he told me.

I nodded, gulping back my range of emotions.

'Where are you staying?' he wanted to know.

'With friends.' Indifferently.

It all flashed through my mind: the support and tolerance of my friends as I worked my way through this emotional minefield; the advances of entirely suitable men who must have wondered what on earth I was doing; the counselling I was undertaking to process what had happened and why; the resolves I'd made about him in his absence; the resolves I'd made about me. They looked different with him standing there.

'Which friends?' he asked, all soft and expectant.

It's over. That's all I have to say. I don't want him to know where I live. I'm safe, out here in public. Tell him the truth. Finish it. But look at him standing there all sweet and hopeful. How could I break his heart?

I was scared of him too. He'd come after me. He'd find me. It was better to appease him and keep him nice.

'With Brenda.'

He looked pleased. He liked Brenda.

As soon as it was out of my mouth, I regretted it but he knew now, so I had to let him come back with me.

Scotty came and went from the rambling old Eastsider opposite the river that I shared with Brenda and several others. I worked during the day as a teacher. He went off and did whatever it was he did. The evenings were fun and satisfying with whoever was around – the two of us and various others: cross-cultural socialising in Alice Springs in the late 1980s.

I enjoyed Scotty's company and went along with his idea that we were partners but I knew it wasn't right. At the same time, I continued to have counselling with the ultimate aim of understanding my role in this dysfunctional relationship and extricating myself from it for good.

During that time, snuggled up together at night, Scotty said to me, 'Let's make a baby.'

Young and healthy, with maternal hormones kicking around my body, I swooned at the thought. There was nothing I wanted more. I knew the circumstances weren't ideal but since when I had let less than ideal circumstances stand in the way?

It was fine and fun for weeks. Scotty came and went a bit but I didn't mind. I enjoyed his company and so did my friends. It was a vibrant, happy household. Scotty's insecurity reared its head sometimes and I was always a little bit on guard, keeping him happy, saying the things I knew were good for keeping the peace. Even when we were being as partners, even when I was telling him I loved him, deep down I knew this couldn't last. During the times that he went away, I enjoyed the easier way of being with just my friends.

One afternoon, Scotty turned up with that look and smell like he'd been drinking and trouble was a-brewing. I met him out the front.

'Who've you been sleeping with?' he demanded.

For goodness sake. Here we go again.

'No one, Scotty. I've been waiting for you.'

'No. who've you been with? I just want to know. I'll walk away now.'

There was a menacing tension. I knew he wouldn't walk away. Anyway, I hadn't been sleeping with anyone. The whole situation was ludicrous.

Then thwack. The fist. I recoiled.

Ashley, Brenda's boyfriend, was out the front in a flash. He put himself between Scotty and me. 'You don't hit girls,' he stated, like that was the surest and most obvious thing on earth.

Suddenly people came from everywhere, the whole extended household. They formed a circle around me with Scotty on the outside, like a child's game, only this one wasn't for fun.

Every time Scotty made a move or tried to open his mouth, Ashley repeated, calmly but firmly, 'You don't hit girls.'

This lasted for about twenty minutes, then Scotty walked off down the street.

That night, I packed up and moved on. I didn't want Scotty to know where I lived. I was done with him, breaking up for good. My friends supported my decision and helped me carry my things out to the car.

I rented a room at Lisa's. I kept teaching, continued counselling and worked at getting my life and mind back in order.

Then one day Scotty walked up to me outside the post office, outside the parcel hatch amidst the gathering throng. I'd been part of that too, until he stood there in front of me, with hope written all over his dear, familiar face. I hadn't seen him for several weeks. I was thrilled and terrified in equal measure...

'Allo,' he said, standing there almost sheepishly, "Ow are you?' That high-pitched, endearing voice.

'I'm okay.'

'I've missed you.'

I nodded, gulping back my range of emotions.

'Where are you staying?'

'With friends.'

'Which friends?' he asked keenly, like he was a part of my life.

It's over. That's all I have to say. I don't want him to know where I live… But look at him standing there all dear and hopeful. How could I break his heart like that?

'With Lisa.'

He looked pleased. He liked Lisa.

As soon as it was out of my mouth I regretted it but I let him come back with me.

That night, Scotty brought up what had happened last time we'd seen each other. 'Why did they all stand around you like that?' he asked.

'Because they were protecting me.'

'Well, that's none of their business. A lot of men hit their wives. That's between them. It's no one else's business. If a man hits his wife, it means he loves her.'

*

I was like a junkie. Scotty was my fix. At those times of reunion, when we hugged, I felt an overwhelming sense of relief. He was happy. He loved me. For a moment, all was fine. Then, as soon as that was over, as soon as I'd let him back in, I kicked myself. It happened half a dozen times over the next twelve months. But I kept up with my counselling, kept reading books on co-dependency and coming to terms with my condition. A few steps forward, then the odd stumble backwards.

*

There were times when I moved on and wasn't seeing him. And then there were times when he knew where I lived and was around. During one of those times, Scotty had some legal trouble, an alcohol-related offence. His lawyer asked me to appear in court as a character witness. I wore my favourite frock, black splashed with pretty pink rosebuds, that I'd bought from Wayne's Indonesian clothing in the Todd Mall. It was comfortably wash and wear and looked good, even on the roughest days. I stood up in the dock and explained to the court that I was Scotty's girlfriend, he was a nice guy with a drinking problem and I didn't think that another spell in jail would do him any good.

The Alice Springs court system is clogged with Aboriginal men who have committed alcohol-related offences. Some of them, like my old friend and teaching assistant Joe Daniels, welcome their time in jail. Others, like Scotty, loathe it. The jail is full to bursting of men who go in and out, on a revolving-door basis. The situation has been the same for decades and the official name 'Correctional Centre' is a bit of a joke when the same guys keep ending up back inside.

The magistrate, constrained by the system, handed down another small sentence.

I wrote Scotty letters and visited him. The jail was as quaint as such an institution can be; a relic from a bygone era. Made of stone and concrete, it was built initially in 1938 to house sixteen prisoners. By 1991 it was majorly overcrowded and outdated, perhaps like the system that sustained it.

Visiting time was Saturday morning. You turned up at the front gate and pressed the buzzer.

'Yes,' a bored voice boomed through the speaker in the wall.

'I'm here to see Barney Scott,' I would say with as much conviction as I could muster.

'Name?' the voice commanded.

'Linda Wells.'

'Take a seat.'

By a seat he meant a perch on the lawn amongst fellow jail visitors. I knew quite a few of them, mostly people who had made the journey in from the bush to see their husbands/sons/fathers.

'Miss Kumenjayi, you coming to see that *Jungarrayi*?'

'*Yuwayi*.'

'Come. Sit down with us.'

I moved easily in this world and valued my place, not as a social worker or prison screw but just as a fellow human being.

As visitors trickled out through the gates, names were called for the next on the list to go in. An hour passed, maybe two, sitting in the sunshine, having a chat, laughing at the irrepressible enthusiasm of the kids and waiting for your name to be called.

For many of the bush people, jail was just a fact of life, a rite of passage or something you got resigned to. Many young men did at least one stint in jail during the course of their coming of age. Visiting a loved one doing time was something that those of us connected to them did.

When my name was called, I went in through the iron gates and was frisked. My bag went into a locker, to be retrieved on the way out. I had no other experience of jails, except from films and literature, but it seemed like a low-level country kind of jail and not too foreboding. The visiting area was outdoors undercover, concrete with old wooden tables and chairs. There was room for about fifteen visitors at a time.

Scotty came through in his green prison T-shirt, looking healthy and rather pleased with himself. The prisoners wore T-shirts in a range of fashion colours. Most wore green, the colour allocated to low-risk detainees. There was yellow for those on remand, blue for medium-term and red for the highest risk and most serious convicted criminals. Even though he didn't like being there, jail seemed to suit Scotty. He was always happy to see me, with a big grin on his face, and was clean, well-rested and sober.

The best laid plans of mice and men originate in jail. Scotty loved me. He wanted to be a worthy partner and for us to have a good life together. He was giving up the devil grog. He was going to reform, concentrate on his music, and get some training and a job. I was seduced by his intentions even though some solid part of me knew it was an impossible, fuzzy dream.

'Yes, darling,' I'd say, but it was like we each had the fingers of one hand crossed behind our backs.

I was bound to Scotty in some curious and powerful way. It was a product of my recklessly adventurous spirit, an eroded self-esteem, an addiction or a heady mixture of the lot.

Scotty got out on Christmas Eve 1991. I have a photo of him on the front lawn of Liz's house that I was minding at the time. He's glowing with health and happiness, beaming proudly and holding up a teapot in place of a can of VB. Eventually the teapot was replaced by a can of VB and we reverted to the push-me-pull-you cycle.

*

I continued with my counselling. I explored my behavioural roots and the theory of co-dependence. It fitted comfortably. I put other people's needs first. I was so damned empathetic that I could see someone else's point of view more clearly than my own. My self-protective mechanisms were out of order and what I had been through, the violence and the fear, exacerbated the condition and further undermined my self-esteem.

Seeing it clearly was one thing. Managing it was another. I knew I could flee at any time, jump on a train and return down south, walk away and start a new life. I had so many more options than the multitudes of other women I knew in Central Australia who suffered from the similar deranged and twisted attentions of their partners. But I knew I had a condition that I had to figure out and that you can't run away from yourself.

I know a man should never hit a woman nor visa versa. Domestic and family violence are inexcusable. Scotty's behaviour was horrible, his insecurities and possessiveness and the violence that resulted. But despite the signs that emerged early in our relationship, the STIs, the jealousy and possessiveness, I kept going back. I had a role to play in the terrible dysfunction.

I had a counsellor, Suzanne M— who worked from the Health and Relaxation Centre amongst the other psychics and alternatives. Just entering that centre felt therapeutic and other-worldly, with its sweet fragrances, its tinkling water feature, crystals and affirmations all around. Such spaciness was in contrast to the earthed tones of the life I had been leading. Out bush, there were also mystics, spiritual healers and approaches to life and well-being that went way beyond the physical, but out bush you felt grounded, on the earth. The Health and Relaxation Centre was focused on the stars.

Suzanne was light and pure, like an angel. She wore loose, lightly coloured clothes and each time she guided me from the waiting room into her private chambers, I breathed a deep sigh of relief.

'Linda, come in. How are you?' She smoothed out the towels that covered the massage table and helped me to get settled, lying on my back with one pillow under my head and another under my knees, adjusted until I was comfortable.

Suzanne gave me reiki then, holding her hands over parts of my body, to hover in the aura space that's immediately next to your body without touching it. She held her hands in one place for a while then when the time felt right she moved on to a different part of my body. For an hour, she went around like this, holding her hands close to my body and saying wise and caring things for me to focus on as I lay there.

I don't know how it worked but it did. I always came out of Suzanne's sessions floating, like she'd given me a really good drug. That feeling lasted for an hour or so then gradually wore off. What remained, though, was a feeling of strength and resolve that grew as time went on.

Suzanne told me I was co-dependent and that she was co-dependent too. I couldn't believe it of her. She seemed like the most holistically healthy person I had ever met. She told me you never stop being co-dependent. It's like an addiction and you have to learn to manage it.

It did feel like an addiction. In the part of the cycle where I'd moved along again and got myself free, I was strong and clear for a while but then I would start to crave. I'd see him and feel a powerful need that was tied up with being loved and also making him feel okay. Hugging him would be like a fix, there on the streets of Alice. At times, I even sought him out.

The hug, the kiss, aah, sweet relief; the beautiful, shocking fix; then I'd tell him where I was living. In five minutes, I'd regret it but by then he knew where he could find me. He latched on tight and the cycle had kicked over once again.

*

I knew that I would only be free when I could face up to Scotty and tell him, with words and every other part of my being, that I didn't want to be with him any more.

I had moved a fair way forward but I wasn't quite there. And then the final incentive: a visit to the doctor, a clinical consulting room, a routine test, a result.

'It's positive,' she said like she was telling me I had cancer. The doctor knew my circumstances; she had treated me for the STIs. 'You're pregnant. What are you going to do?' She must have mistaken my audible gasp for something other than sheer pleasure.

'I'm going to have a baby,' I squealed, loud and proud and overjoyed. I was ready and I wanted that more than anything else in the world. I was strong and capable. I would make it work.

She eyed me doubtfully and then said to me, 'Are you sure? There are enough unwanted half-caste children in this town.'

*

Twenty years later, I told my daughter that story; my beautiful, talented, much-loved daughter. I told her those words that even now bring tears to my eyes.

'Where?' she asked, shaking her head. 'Show me the unwanted half-caste children in Alice Springs.'

If there were any, she certainly wasn't one of them.

www.ingramcontent.com/pod-product-compliance
Lightning Source LLC
Chambersburg PA
CBHW030907080526
44589CB00010B/188